State Officials and Higher Education

A SURVEY OF THE OPINIONS AND EXPECTATIONS
OF POLICY MAKERS IN NINE STATES

by *Heinz Eulau*

Professor of Political Science, Stanford University

and *Harold Quinley*

Postdoctoral Fellow, University of California, Berkeley

with a commentary by *David D. Henry*

A General Report Prepared for
The Carnegie Commission on Higher Education

MCGRAW-HILL BOOK COMPANY

New York   St. Louis   San Francisco   Dusseldorf
London   Sydney   Toronto   Mexico   Panama

The Carnegie Commission on Higher Education,
1947 Center Street, Berkeley, California 94704,
has sponsored preparation of this report as a
part of a continuing effort to present significant
information and issues for public discussion.
The views expressed are those of the authors.

STATE OFFICIALS AND HIGHER EDUCATION

A Survey of the Opinions and Expectations of
Policy Makers in Nine States

Library of Congress catalog card number 70–108611

123456789 MAMM 79876543210
          10009

Foreword

The 50 states provide the basic support for colleges and universities that enroll 70.6 percent of all students in the United States. Their financial subsidies and policies are thus crucial to the welfare of higher education in the United States. How do legislative leaders view higher education today? This study by Professor Heinz Eulau and Harold Quinley gives answers to this question, and these answers will help guide future developments. These answers show:

- A great faith in higher education that gave rise to a tripling of expenditures over the past decade.

- An awareness that parent-constituents want educational opportunities for their children.

- An interstate competition for a prestige system of higher education that is a major factor for progress in many states.

- Strong support for public service activities of colleges and universities in solving problems that affect the welfare of the state and its people.

- A favorable attitude toward long-range planning of higher education and centralized coordination as a means of making good use of resources and of expressing the will of the state government.

- A welcoming approach to federal aid with a preference that it be spent through state governments.

- Strong support for community colleges.

- An attitude of caution toward state support for private colleges and universities.

- A substantial degree of understanding of student dissent but a clear preference for a firm hand in dealing with it.

Overall, it is clear that many legislators keep themselves well informed about higher education and consider its support among their highest duties. That they do so is one of the great sources of strength of higher education in the United States.

Clark Kerr

*Chairman
The Carnegie Commission
on Higher Education*

September, 1969

Contents

Introduction

American state legislators are strategic decision makers in policies affecting higher education. The resources mobilized for colleges and universities, the goals to which such resources are allocated, and how they are distributed depend to a great extent on the views and decisions of the nation's legislative bodies. Legislators intervene in higher education not only through conscious planning but also through the inadvertent consequences of legislative action, or inaction, in such related areas of public commitment as agriculture, mental health, social welfare, and defense.

The Carnegie Commission on Higher Education asked us to survey how legislators and certain state executive officials perceived the problems and issues of higher education, their attitudes toward various aspects of higher education, and their expectations of future development. We accepted the assignment willingly, not only in the belief that social service is a duty of the university scholar but also because we thought such information could be valuable to educational administrators and governing boards. In addition, we believed the survey would be useful in pinpointing at least some of the problems that beset the political process, and especially the legislative process, and which in turn create problems for higher education.

This is a report, not a study. The distinction may seem trivial, but only if the intent of our work is clear can it be properly assessed. The questions we asked of public officials were not enlightened by theoretical considerations because we did not seek a representative sample of respondents in the technical sense, because we did not subject our information to systematic analysis, and because we did not see the report as fitting the structure of scientific knowledge. The guidelines given us, and our resources, precluded a systematic and scientific study. This is not to say that we did not try to give our survey and report intellectual stature. The questions asked were influenced by prior knowledge of legislative behavior, the respondents we sought out were not arbitrarily chosen, and our presentation of what we learned is, we hope, informative, objective, and constructive.

Because we were less interested in learning about the distribution of officials' perceptions and attitudes toward higher education and more in assessing their quality, we conducted fairly intensive interviews of a highly selected group of respondents in only a few states.

CHOICE OF STATES

Our choice of states was determined by the need for some with large, complex systems of higher education and for others with less developed systems. The states were to be located in different regions of the country. They were to have legislatures in session during winter-spring 1968. And they were to be states where we could obtain scholars with experience in the legislative process and in interviewing public officials.

Finally selected were states with complex educational systems: California (West), Texas (Southwest), Illinois (Midwest), New York and Pennsylvania (East); and with less complex systems: Iowa and Kansas (Midwest), Kentucky (Border) and Louisiana (South).

All the five larger systems had made substantial percentage gains in appropriations of state tax funds for operating expenses of higher education over the period 1960-1968: New York, 449 percent; Pennsylvania, 245 percent; Illinois, 233.5 percent; Texas, 229.5 percent; and California, 183 percent. Among the less developed systems, Kentucky showed the substantial gain of 397.25 percent. The other three showed substantial if smaller increases: Iowa, 147.5 percent; Kansas, 135.5 percent; and Louisiana, 132.5 percent (Office of Institutional Research, 1968). The five larger systems ranked among the eight states that, in 1966, received the most federal aid for higher education. The other four states ranked as follows on the list of federal grants: Louisiana, twenty-second; Kentucky, twenty-fourth; Iowa, twenty-seventh; Kansas, twenty-ninth (National Science Foundation, 1966).

CHOICE OF RESPONDENTS

For the interviews, we sought legislators most intimately connected with legislation or appropriations for higher education, such as chairmen of education and finance committees and floor leaders. Some respondents were recommended as especially informed about or interested in higher education. Our goal was to interview 10 legislators and 2 executive officials in each of the nine states. As it turned out, we interviewed slightly fewer. Forty-nine of the legislators were Democrats and thirty-nine Republicans. Of the executive officials, seven were Democrats and seven Republicans. Specifically, the roster of respondents had the characteristics indicated in the accompanying tables.

State legislators or staff	
Speakers or presidents pro-tem	10
Majority or minority floor leaders, caucus chairmen	17
Chairmen or vice-chairmen of committees on education, labor, or welfare	19
Chairmen or vice-chairmen of committees on finance, taxation, appropriation, budget, etc.	12
Ranking members of education committees	12
Ranking members of finance committees	11
Other legislators	5
Legislative staff personnel involved in higher education	2
TOTAL	88

State executive officials	
Governors or lieutenant governors	4
Budget directors or finance directors	4
Commissioners or superintendents of education	3
Assistants to governors	3
TOTAL	14

The limited, but by no means arbitrary, nature of the sample precluded making exact distributive statements about the attitudes and perceptions of American state legislators, executive officials, or even legislative leaders. We shall therefore be dealing in types and themes, remaining largely mute on questions of distribution, although we shall sometimes use such words as *many, some,* or *few.* But not much weight should be given to these apparently quantitative expressions. It should also be remembered that the respondents chosen were more knowledgeable about higher education than the average legislator and probably more sympathetic to its needs. Thus their views cannot be considered representative within the legislature as a whole, but may be more supportive than those of the average legislator.

Because the interview was designed to be exploratory, the questions included in the schedule (Appendix A) were intentionally open-ended. Even if they did become specific, especially in probing, their purpose was primarily to serve as stimuli to move the conversation along. The questions were not designed to elicit factual information available elsewhere. Therefore, even if the respondent misunderstood a question, interviewers were instructed to let him speak freely because it was thought that his interpretation of a question might itself be of interest. But interviewers were also asked, in this case, to return to the original question by subtly reformulating it.

The objective of the interview, then, was not a reconstruction of the actual educational situation in state or nation, but a description of it as the respondent defined it. We were interested in discovering his assumptions, perceptions, attitudes, and expectations. The interviewers were especially asked never to give the impression that the respondent's knowledge was being tested. Interviewers were encouraged to provide the respondent with facts (if they were sure of them) in order to see how he reacted, but when probing they were to use such phrases as "generally speaking," "overall," "from what you can judge," and so on.

The interviewers were also instructed to adjust inquiries to the particular conditions in a state. Although it was hoped that they might cover all questions, they were free to pursue lines that seemed of particular interest or within the special competence of the respondent. In any case, because it was not our intention to discover the distribution of attitudes or perceptions, exploration "in depth" was preferred to superficial answers.

Finally, although the questions were largely worded to elicit the respondent's own views, it was suggested to the interviewers to ask, where it seemed especially appropriate, how "others" felt about a given matter. This, it seemed to us, might yield some interesting, even if unreliable, information.

For the kind of freewheeling interview we proposed to conduct, we could not rely on the run-of-the-mill survey interviewer employed by polling agencies or even on graduate students. We needed the help of professional political scientists who were well acquainted with the legislative process and the politics of the states and were capable of conducting the kind of interview that required much "thinking on one's feet." This made interviewing quite expensive, but we succeeded in attracting to the project a group of colleagues whom we could entrust with a task that required much discretion.

A first draft of the interview schedule was developed in collaboration with the staff of the Commission and Professor Robert H. Salisbury of Washington University. This draft was carefully reviewed by the whole group of interviewers in Chicago in January, 1968. Because the schedule was chiefly thought of as an aid in interviewing and as a guide to the kind of topics to be covered, it was felt that a pretest, conventional in more systematic interviewing, was not necessary.

Once respondents had been selected (by our field interviewers), they were informed about the nature of the project in a letter from Dr. Clark Kerr, the chairman of the Carnegie Commission (Appendix B), and asked to cooperate with the project. The interviewers made their own arrangements for the interviews, and most were conducted in March and April, 1968, though a few were not finished until the end of June. Only one legislator refused to be interviewed, although some governors and other high officials could not be reached.

Most of the interviews were recorded on tape, which, it seemed to us, would provide a verbatim transcript of content, tone, and degree of emphasis considerably superior to any other form of recording. A memorandum on interviewing by tape was prepared for us by Professor Robert Peabody of Johns Hopkins University (who conducted a number of interviews in Congress not included in this report). In the few cases where respondents preferred not being taped, the interviewers were instructed to take as full notes as possible and to fill out each interview from memory immediately upon its conclusion.

All respondents were assured of complete anonymity, both in the letter of invitation and at the beginning of each interview. We hope that we have protected each respondent's privacy in our report.

The interviews averaged about 1 hour and 15 minutes, though several took as long as 2 hours. Most of the respondents were cooperative, although they differed a great deal in candor. On the whole, most of the interviews were successfully completed.

Although the taped interview has many virtues, it creates formidable problems for review and use of the material. In the first place, 102 interviews transcribed from tape to paper yield several thousand pages of text that must be read before anything else can be done. Second, because of the freewheeling nature of the interview process, the interviews did not follow as much as one might have hoped the order of the questions on the schedule. As a result, each interview had to be indexed in terms of categories to make the task of selecting relevant sections manageable. Third, once this task had been completed, it was still necessary to make selections from the various categoric parts into which each interview had been divided. Many of the statements from one interview to the next were repetitive, and because we were primarily interested in the best interpretations of a problem or an attitude, each interview had to be combed for the most useful material. Finally, as most of our respondents were politicians, who cannot be easily dissuaded from expressing whatever comes to mind or from telling anecdotes only remotely related to the subject of an interview, much of what was recorded was of no use at all.

Our strategy was largely to let our respondents speak for themselves. This, it seemed to us, followed from our decision to tape the interviews in the first place. The bulk of the report is a kind of edited primary document rather than a summary of what the respondents told our interviewers. We sought to select quotations from the interviews which, in some respects, were typical of the ideas of many, some, or few respondents, but which, in other respects, were quite atypical in the sense that they were the best, i.e., the most explicit or detailed statements of a point of view or perception. Although we tried to be as objective as possible in selecting materials from the interviews and by giving examples of various positions that respondents took on matters of higher education, we cannot guarantee that any of the quotations are in any way truly representative of what legislators and other officials see, think, or feel.

In presenting the relevant materials we have sought, in respect to many topics, to develop a kind of composite profile of what our respondents had on their minds, regardless of the particular conditions that surrounded particular perceptions or attitudes. We can assume that what a respondent told us was influenced by a multitude of circumstances—the particular nature of the educational system, economic and political conditions in a state, the respondent's objective knowledge or ignorance, position occupied in the legislative process, personal experiences, political predispositions, length of tenure in office, and so on.

Because of the nature of the interview, we were in no position to relate such variables to responses in order to explain variances in answers from state to state, party to party, house to house, committee to committee, or person to person. In general, we have indicated the respondent's state in introducing examples from the interviews and occasionally his formal position or party affiliation. But while such identification may at times shed some light on what is said, it cannot be assumed to explain it. In other words, the materials presented in this report must largely speak for themselves. They do tell us a great deal, certainly, about how political minds think about higher education, and they can give the reader a feeling for the variety of points of view, but they cannot tell us much about either their causes or consequences.

All this is not to say that we have eschewed appraisal altogether. Where the evidence was overwhelming, in favor or opposition to a policy, we have said so without counting noses. Where we had some evaluation to make, we have done so. But we have tried not to impose our own views on the material, or to use the material to promote personal points of view. The document here presented, we hope, will be of some use to those who wish to know how political men assess the problems and prospects of higher education in the third quarter of the century.

1. State Patterns: Background to Interviews

As background for our composite profile of legislators' attitudes, we asked our *interviewers* to report on and evaluate the systems of higher education existing in the nine states. The comments of legislators and state officials can be more readily and meaningfully assessed within the framework of the material presented in this chapter.

As might be expected, even our interviewers saw and emphasized quite different things. Some of our collaborators stressed the politics of the state as it seemed to them to affect higher education. Others emphasized administrative developments in the state's system of higher education; and still others, the social and economic constraints or opportunities that appeared to them as crucial components of problems in higher education. What follows, then, are highlights of the structural, geographic, economic, political, and personality factors our interviewers thought relevant to an understanding of higher education in their respective states when the interviews were conducted.

CALIFORNIA   Decision making for public higher education in California has involved perhaps the most persistent and intense conflicts of any area of state policy in recent years. Especially appropriation battles — primarily for support of the University of California and the state colleges — are annual events in the Legislature. In part, the intensity of this conflict stems from the status of higher education as the most expensive item among the nondedicated expenditures of the state. In spring, 1968, this area accounted for almost 40 percent of the budget subject to complete legislative scrutiny. Funding decisions for higher education thus frequently reflect and affect decisions on taxes and other revenue sources. This relationship became clearer than ever in 1967 when a Republican administration pledged to economy and tax relief came into office along with a Democratic-controlled Legislature relatively sympathetic to requests for higher levels of funding for the University and colleges. The result was a series of deadlocks on the 1967 legislative budget, particularly in the areas of higher education and mental hygiene where the greatest cuts from agency requests were made by the administration.

Throughout 1967 and 1968 the administration and Democratic legislators differed on the revenue sources appropriate to support greater funding for higher education. Governor Reagan emphasized tuition charges for students; the Democrats stressed withholding of state income taxes as a means of solving a number of funding problems. The resolution of this dispute was complicated by the legal ability of the administration and Legislature to legislate student charges only for the colleges, the University enjoying constitutional autonomy in this area. In April, 1968, after more than a year of discussion, the regents adopted an $81 annual "University registration fee" increase. While only a small portion of the funds so raised was to be used for general University expenditures, this was regarded as a symbolic victory for the Governor, a precedent for future increased student charges, and a stimulus for the Legislature to enact similar charges at the state colleges.

Formally, the higher education budget proceeds from the recommendations of the University and college administrations to their governing boards, to the governor and his Department of Finance, to the Senate Finance and Assembly Ways and Means Committees, to the full Legislature, and to the governor for the signing of the overall budget document. The process is informally characterized by a great deal of negotiation, particularly between representatives of the institutions, departments of finance, and the legislative analyst. The major dispute involves the funding of new programs and increased faculty and nonacademic positions.

There are separate budget items for the University and colleges for operating expenditures, capital spending, and salary increases; and each of these items often generates conflict. The state's budget also contains relatively small sums for support of junior colleges and for scholarship aid to students at private institutions.

Numerous strains exist within the California complex of public higher education, particularly concerning the roles desired by the various institutions. The California Master Plan for Higher Education, enacted in 1960, established separate responsibilities for the

University, state colleges, and junior colleges. This allocation of functions has been consistently challenged, primarily by the state colleges, which regard the 1960 plan as merely a holding action. They have sought to share in the University's virtual monopolies on research and graduate education, to move further from their pre-1960 position as essentially teacher-training campuses. On its part the University has protected its status by resisting the development of new state college programs.

The state's junior colleges were assigned missions by the 1960 master plan as largely vocational and freshman-sophomore institutions serving local communities. This reflected the origin of the older junior colleges as operations of local school districts and adjuncts of high schools. But with a great increase in the number of junior colleges in recent years, stimulated by legislation requiring all parts of the state to be organized into junior college districts, this segment of California higher education also has been chafing at its assigned role. A major conflict is over state funds. The junior colleges now are primarily supported by local property taxes, with relatively small amounts of state aid for capital outlay. Some junior colleges favor greatly expanded state aid for operations as a means of eliminating local voter control over finances, while others oppose this because of expected state control.

One potential umpire in these jurisdictional battles, the Coordinating Council for Higher Education, has not performed in this role. Established by the 1960 plan, this agency has been more of an advisory and informational body than one attempting to control or coordinate the actions of the various components of California higher education.

The governing structures and procedures of the several institutions have involved other conflicts. The ability of the University's board of regents to protect this institution from outside political pressures has been questioned by some, in part because of the board's dismissal of the president in early 1967. Others comment that the regents are not responsive enough to public opinion and to the executive and legislative branches. At any rate, the regents' meetings since early 1967 have been arenas of dispute and confrontation, primarily between factions led by Governor Reagan and liberal Democratic appointees.

As state legislatures go, the California body is both innovative and demanding. It is more than a translator of inputs: a high proportion of changes in state policies and programs originate in the work of legislative committees and members. That higher education is affected by this innovative quality was exemplified by the creation of the Joint Committee on Higher Education in 1965. The committee, with five members from each house, is reviewing a wide range of matters, including possible changes in the 1960 master plan and funding options. Much legislative innovation, however, is characterized by the introduction of bills intended to punish public higher education for policies or occurrences that offend the public. Those have little chance at passage. Legislative proposals of this sort in 1968 included bills to forbid Communist speakers on campuses, to control the content of student dramatic productions, and to establish statewide University and college police agencies.

The demanding aspect of the California Legislature concerns the expectations members have as to the quality of representations made before them. They demand information and openness, particularly from public agencies at budget time. On this account legislators of both political parties and in both houses have been critical of the way higher education institutions make and justify requests. The University in particular has been accused of "academic arrogance" in recent years because of its alleged refusal to explain its needs to the satisfaction of individual legislators.

Few University and state college campuses in California over the past three years have been immune to student demonstrations. While the most violent events have taken place on the urban campuses at Berkeley and San Francisco, even such bucolic places as Davis and Chico have experienced demonstrations against Dow Chemical and the draft. The campus unrest has had obvious impacts on the general community. Newspaper editorials, letters to legislators, and angry speeches by public officials have resulted. Public higher education in California is a controversial matter.

Condensed from a report by
Professor Alvin D. Sokolow,
University of California,
Davis, May, 1968.

ILLINOIS Higher education in Illinois has been brought into a highly structured state system. The system is characterized by extensive planning, and the desires and plans of the individual college and university units are coordinated and controlled by the Board of Higher Education.

The Board of Higher Education was created by statute in 1961 to serve as the central coordinating and planning mechanism for all public institutions of higher education in Illinois. It is composed of 16 members: the presidents or chairmen of each of the five boards which direct the five institutional systems of higher education, including the regency universities, Southern Illinois University, the state colleges and universities, the University of Illinois, and the junior colleges; 10 public members appointed by the governor with consent of the Senate for overlapping six-year terms; and the state superintendent of public instruction. The board has a modest but highly trained staff which has produced a heavy flow of documents and analyses of each activity of each institution down to the individual course and highly sophisticated studies of space utilization. The board functions for many of its purposes through a welter of ad hoc committees to which are coopted numbers of citizens from significant interest groups in the state, from various sections of the state, and from college and university faculties and administrations, public and private.

The board is charged with three principal types of responsibility. First, it was directed to develop a master plan. Phase I of this plan was completed in 1964 and phase II in 1966. Additional major studies are under way which will be worked into revision, elaboration, and updating of the master plan.

Second, the board has authority to review all university budget requests, both capital and operating budgets, and to make recommendations to the governor and the General Assembly. Although this power is advisory only, in fact the several universities have ultimately accepted the advice of the board. Consequently, in the last three biennia the actual requests from the university heads were precisely in line with board recommendations. It seems that norms have quickly developed which confer upon the board effective power to coordinate and adjust higher education budgets as to both total amounts and proportionate shares allocated to the various components of the system.

The third charge to the board gives it full legal authority to make decisions. Under the statute the board must review and determine whether to approve any proposed new programs of instruction, research, or service in any state institution. This authority is exercised; for example, in December, 1967, the board approved six new doctoral programs and disapproved one. Nevertheless, such authority can only obtain for new programs and cannot by itself be a device by which the board reviews existing activities. The board's budget review may be significant for this purpose, but inevitably must be, and is, used with discretion.

Since the board's creation, the passage of several federal programs affecting higher education has brought additional responsibilities. The board serves as the state administrative unit for programs requiring such a central mechanism, and it prepares the state plans. For example, in administering Higher Education Facilities Act grants, it reviews grant applications from public and private institutions, assigns priorities, and makes recommendations to the U.S. Office of Education.

There seems little doubt that the board has quickly come to dominate much of the decision-making process respecting Illinois higher education. It makes the effective budget review, and is at present the only agency which does so. The board's recommendations regarding the number, type, and location of new state universities have prevailed. Its strategies for adjusting the claims of established state universities and new ones, of public institutions and the private sector, and of the other contending interests in the system have been successful thus far, almost without exception.

But there are signs of unhappiness. In part, these come from spokesmen for particular institutions who feel their alma maters have been relegated to lesser status in the process of expansion. Not a little of this sentiment is held by those identifying with the University of Illinois at Urbana, and their resentment is directed toward the board in general and its executive director in particular. In the Legislature, generally, the feeling is widespread that the board has taken over the decision making so completely and with such competence that the Legislature as an institution is threatened and must take steps to reassert its primacy, mainly by means of additional staff help.

Whatever the future may hold, the present Board of Higher Education plays a powerful role. One may ask how so new an agency has achieved such hegemony in its field. In considering the question, we may observe at least three factors in addition to the not unimportant legal authority the board possesses.

First, the board has taken the Legislature and the governor off the hook. In an era of fantastic expansion in higher education the board has made all the hard decisions regarding priorities and interinstitutional allocations, and it has done so with both generosity (recommending major increases each biennium) and prudence (reducing requests substantially, introducing cost studies and space utilization analysis). The board has high credibility, therefore, and can be deferred to with confidence by nearly every legislator. Only legislators who are aggrieved by the board's treatment of their constituencies are unhappy, and these are a small minority.

Second, the board has provided effective support for a major expansion of public higher education in the Chicago area. It is strongly urban-oriented in its educational philosophy. In addition, by relying heavily on demographic analyses for guiding location decisions, the board can hardly avoid stressing the expansion of facilities in the Chicago area. This orientation wins important support in the Legislature. Illinois was long a prime example of rural-dominated, malapportioned politics, and Chicago interests did not loom large in the capitol. But in the 1960s, the governor was a Chicago Democrat. Cook County and environs have greatly enlarged representation, much of it Republican, but all of it supportive of more higher education in the Chicago area.

The third factor is the personnel appointed to the Board of Higher Education. If we assume that the representatives of the several governing boards serve largely as spokesmen for their respective institutions, the critical question is what kinds of people serve as public members. We cannot say very much on this issue except to report the impression, conveyed by legislators and by the press, that the public members are distinguished and strong. The staff is directed by a professional social scientist from California, widely acknowledged to have great technical and substantive ability.

Private institutions of higher education play a major role in Illinois. Not only do they account for nearly half of the enrollment in the state, but they offer standards of quality which are acknowledged by many legislators and educators. The private schools have expressed some unhappiness at the creation of additional state universities, but increased state scholarship funds, about 83 percent of which have gone to nonpublic colleges, allayed their anxiety somewhat. The private schools are organized into the Federation of Independent Illinois Colleges and Universities, which has become a major element in the public decision making regarding higher education. Representatives of private colleges serve on nearly every study committee created by the Board of Higher Education, and several elements of the master plan make particular reference to ways and means of strengthening private institutions and enlarging their role. In 1967 the General Assembly authorized a major study

to advise "on how non-public institutions can be appropriately related to the public ones, without impairment of their freedom, and
on constitutional means by which the state can aid the non-public
institutions in the fulfillment of their tasks." The study is being
directed by a group of five distinguished out-of-state educators.

The conjunction of many factors, then, has resulted in a powerful
Board of Higher Education which makes major decisions and plans
for Illinois. The key word is *system,* for what the board has done is
to transform a collection of institutions with different governing
boards, geographically specialized interests, and uncoordinated,
catch-as-catch-can budgeting and appropriations into a state system
with explicit criteria and well-developed data to shape decisions.

Condensed from a report by
Professor Robert H. Salisbury,
Washington University,
May, 1968.

IOWA   Iowa is predominantly Republican and socially homogeneous (less
than 1 percent of the population is black). While the state is changing from a rural- to an urban-oriented society, this is happening
much more slowly than in many other states. As a result there are
no dramatic social cleavages that produce controversy in the political world. The political attitudes of Iowans are neither strongly
conservative, strongly liberal, nor divided: they are just a little to
the right of center. This makes for rather dull, if peaceful, politics.
Higher education both benefits and loses as a consequence.

For instance, education, and presumably higher education, are
valued highly by the people. They would be willing to spend rather
large sums of money on producing an excellent system of education,
at least by the standards of their state. However, this same pride
in higher education would seem to indicate that Iowans already
think that they are doing a good job. There is no indication that
they feel that the investment of large sums of money is necessary to
bring institutions up to a level significantly higher than they have
presently achieved.

More concretely, the operating budget of the state's three major
institutions of higher learning has grown at a faster rate than student enrollment during the 20-year period 1947-1967—from $17.9
million, or approximately $350 per student per year, for the 1947-
1949 biennium to $96.7 million, or approximately $2,300 per year,

for the biennium 1965-1967. Thus, as the enrollment was doubling the per-pupil expenditure by the state increased by more than five times. But the dramatic rise of the operating budget is not paralleled by an equally steady rise in the capital improvement budget. Most building at the three institutions must be financed with state appropriations. Only dormitories and other revenue-producing facilities such as student unions and athletic facilities can be financed with bonds. The low capital improvement budget, in a time when enrollments have doubled, has caused a tight squeeze on office and classroom space.

The state is not the only source of funds for higher education. But unlike other states, conservative Iowa has not gotten its share of the large sums of money invested by the federal government in university facilities and research. This was due, in part at least, to the influence of a former university president. His attitude toward the federal government was that of a typical conservative Republican—you should not get mixed up with the federal government unless it is absolutely necessary. This attitude still seems prevalent among professors on the campus. One hears faculty members speak very seriously in terms of "hard money" (state appropriations) and "soft money" (federal money). Very few professors are willing to draw any substantial part of their own salaries from research grants even if they have the opportunity.

Traditionally, state support for higher education has been limited to the three institutions controlled by the board of regents. There are a number of public junior colleges in the state, but they have received little state aid, their support coming primarily from their communities.

The decade of the sixties has been one of major innovation in higher education in Iowa. In 1965 the Legislature authorized the establishment of up to 20 community colleges that could provide two years of college preparation work and vocational and technical training. This program was proposed by the Governor and most of the preliminary work on the development of the legislation was done by the state Board of Public Instruction. The legislation was passed by large majorities in the Legislature (45 to 12 in the Senate and 113 to 5 in the House).

But community colleges almost immediately ran into difficulties. When the Legislature met in 1967, there was obvious animus. The community colleges had been established much faster than had been anticipated, and a number of charges of mismanagement were made. The debate centered on financing the operation of the community colleges. Opponents argued that they were using deficit financing (a practice specifically prohibited by the constitution of the state) to get established. The friends of the community colleges argued that the apparent deficit was not a real one but the result of the practice specifically used by the state to distribute operating expenses. While the argument of the proponents was probably more accurate than that of the opponents, the heat engendered by the debate clearly indicated that many people thought the Board of Public Instruction had gone too far too fast.

There are 24 private four-year colleges and universities and 5 junior colleges in Iowa. During the 20-year period from 1947 to 1967 these private schools had enrollments totaling close to 50 percent of the total number of students in college in Iowa. In fact, from 1958 to 1966, more students were enrolled in private colleges in Iowa than in the three state universities. With the exception of Grinnell, Coe, and Cornell, the quality of education is probably poor, but they are educating a very large number of young people in Iowa. Financing private higher education is, as in other states, becoming more and more difficult. During the 1967 legislative session the Iowa Association of Private Colleges and Universities began a campaign to get the Legislature to provide support for the private colleges. The association appears to be well organized and during 1968 held meetings with legislators all over the state to present arguments for public support.

While Iowa has made significant advances in supporting higher education in the past few years, major difficulties can be foreseen in the immediate future. The cost of operation and capital improvements at the three state universities is increasing sharply. The full financial impact of the community colleges has not been felt in any significant way. Over the next 10 years the operating budgets of these colleges will have to rise very rapidly if they are to perform the tasks envisioned by the legislators and the planners in the Board of Public Instruction. If the state provides effective support for the private colleges, this will require millions of dollars a year. Then there are the costs of establishing a new four-year college.

However, one has the distinct impression that state officials do not have any clear grasp of the total cost of these programs. Each is treated independently. There seems to be no clear recognition that the state is embarking on programs that could mean a doubling or tripling of state appropriations for higher education. Governor

Hughes has moved on to the United States Senate and is no longer a guiding influence in legislative policy. If the dramatic increase in demand is coupled with a new Republican administration more concerned about keeping taxes low than about expanding higher education, it could mean that state financial aid will be spread too thin and that some or all of these programs will have to be sharply curtailed.

Condensed from a report by
Professor G. Robert Boynton,
University of Iowa,
August, 1968.

KANSAS In general there seems no reason to expect dramatic changes in the size and composition of the Kansas system of higher education in the foreseeable future. The number of institutions will probably remain the same. It is unlikely that Washburn University, the municipal university in Topeka, will be added to the system because of the budgetary problems facing the Legislature and because of the attitude of Washburn administrators and alumni. Preference for self-administration under the municipal charter will likely keep supporters from seeking incorporation in the state system, where Washburn would have to compete with the three established universities.

The future organization and structure of the Kansas system is problematical. Some sentiment exists for the creation of a single administrative structure to oversee all operations. This would involve the creation of the position of president of the universities of Kansas under the state board of regents. The several campuses would be supervised by a separate chancellor directly responsible to the president. It is not clear as to whether the state colleges would be included within this general system, whether they would have their own parallel system as in California, or whether they would remain separate and independent but under the same board of regents. Major reasons in support of the innovation are that it would facilitate integration of higher education and reduce the duplication of functions and programs, especially in graduate training; minimize financial competition in the Legislature; and provide for better planning and liaison with the administrative and legislative branches of government.

The increased demand for higher education is most likely to

affect Wichita State University, especially at the undergraduate level. Dramatic growth would intensify the demand for revenue and serve as an impetus to establish duplicative graduate programs as a complement to the expanded undergraduate program.

Junior colleges present an immediate problem. If they are to be academically oriented, they should be incorporated under the board of regents into the state system to ensure quality and raise academic standards. In general, the 16 existing junior colleges are probably sufficient for current needs.

Graduate programs leading to the Ph.D. pose a long-range problem for Kansas. There are two points of view on the matter, one being that Ph.D. programs should be developed at all three universities since each has its own specialties and proficiencies. The other view is that regardless of past patterns, Ph.D. degrees should be offered under the auspices of the University of Kansas at Lawrence. This view is based on the idea that the University of Kansas graduate school has achieved certain levels of excellence which should not be diluted by the creation of competing programs, especially when costs are taken into consideration.

Professional schools represent another problem. Kansas does not have a dental school but has a reciprocal arrangement with Missouri whereby Kansas residents may use its dental facilities and Missourians may use some other Kansas professional facilities. There is much agreement that professional training should be viewed as a regional responsibility with states entering into bilateral and multilateral reciprocal agreements to meet the high costs.

Increasing costs of medical education are especially of concern to the state. One solution might be a dual-level medical program somewhat analogous to the two levels of nurses' training, the practical and the registered. A technical and less sophisticated level of medical education might produce "practical medical technicians" trained to provide minor medical and surgical services. This would help to meet the increased demand for services and permit some medical training at a reduced cost.

Kansas needs new sources of revenue to finance education and state operations generally. The property tax seems to be at its limit. Increases in sales and income taxes are probably inevitable as the major sources of future revenue. Kansas income tax rates do not normally exceed 5 percent. There is also the possibility of increasing student tuition and fees.

Four-year institutions face competition for state support from two sources: the junior colleges and primary and secondary schools. General education at this point is the more likely competitor. Local school districts must depend on the already overtaxed ad valorem property tax for most of their revenue. There is considerable sympathy for state aid to local school districts in the form of some sort of tax-sharing program. The state is making major efforts in education at this time. In 1968, 63.4 percent of the governor's budget for the spending of general funds excluding user tax revenues (highway funds, for example) was earmarked for all levels of education.

Condensed from a report by
Professor Herman D. Lujan,
University of Kansas,
May, 1968.

KENTUCKY   Kentucky's institutions of higher learning—the University of Kentucky, the four state universities, the community colleges, and others—are probably more closely linked to politics than is the case in the other states included in this report. The leaders of the state universities, in particular, have in recent years been aggressive and ambitious men, most of whom have had ties of one kind or another with political parties or factions.

In recent years the level of support for higher education has risen rapidly. The state has increased massively its funding of the University of Kentucky and other universities and colleges; at the same time it has built a large number of community colleges. One reason for rising support has been the effective job done by the presidents of state universities, and most notably the president of the University of Kentucky. His resignation in 1968, after five years, illustrates some of the problems facing higher education in the state. What made this more than routine was the spate of rumors that he had been forced or requested to resign by the Governor or by the board of trustees. As far as it is possible to tell, the president resigned voluntarily to take a bigger job in California.

On the other hand, the rumors had some validity: the president had been the focus of intense pressure and some persons inside and outside the university were glad to see him go. Within the university, old-time faculty members objected to the speed with which changes had been made and often differed with the direction of the changes.

Opposition from outside came from many sources. The president had firmly resisted efforts by legislators and citizens to have the university impose some kind of curb on campus speakers and meetings. There were obvious rivalries with state colleges that led to some opposition.

The Main Chance Farm controversy—a dispute over land that placed the university directly in the center of a bitter struggle among powerful financial groups in Lexington—made enemies for the institution and its president. As a result, an antitrust suit was brought against the university. A legislative audit committee investigated the affair, and the Legislature then passed bills designed to regulate the activities of the university's purchasing agency.

The university is a powerful force in Lexington, as other universities are in their cities. Its activities, and particularly its plans regarding property in the community, can have a marked impact on the economy. If local interests have political power and are prepared to use it, the university can be damaged, its goals can be frustrated, its freedom to act and even its budget can be restricted.

Apart from leadership within the educational establishment, a major factor in the university's growth has been the favorable attitude of governors since 1959. The Governor has been the dominant force in the budgetary process. His budgets have been accepted consistently by legislatures with little or no change.

In the 1968 session, Governor Nunn won support for an increase in the sales tax to 5 percent to finance his larger budget. It is noteworthy that the Kentucky Education Association provided massive support for passage of both Nunn's budget and his tax program without change.

Primary-secondary education supporters have more influence in the Legislature than do supporters of higher education. The teachers' groups have more contacts with the average legislator than do representatives of higher education. Moreover, as the last two governors have demonstrated, the chief executive is highly susceptible to pressure from school groups. However, there is some evidence of growing resistance of legislators to the Kentucky Education Association. Some of them are beginning to suggest that the state cannot indefinitely carry such a large share (70 percent) of the cost of local education.

Governor Nunn has maintained, though probably not accelerated, the pace of expansion of higher education in the state. By any standard, however, higher education has made great progress in Kentucky in the last decade. Its major universities are much stronger, and the community system has reached into every corner of the state. Judged by physical plant, salaries, enrollment, and the quality of education, the higher education system is much more vigorous than it was a decade ago. A relatively poor state has invested very heavily in higher education—largely because of the initiative of governors. Higher education has strong support in the state and in the Legislature, but the advances that have been made result in part from the Legislature's habit of approving budgets with little or no change. To the extent that legislative review of the budget becomes more thorough, it is possible that controversy over how to spend the educational dollar might become more intensive.

Higher education faces several major problems in Kentucky in the years ahead. The crucial question is the extent to which a relatively poor state can keep up with the growing costs and with the increasingly expensive competition of higher education in other states. The state has just adopted the highest sales tax without exemptions in the country, and there will be strong resistance to any further tax increase in the next several years. Legislators support higher education, but they are going to be looking for "frills" that can be eliminated. It seems probable that some of the costs of graduate and professional education and research at the major universities will be most vulnerable to such economy drives. As the various universities compete for prestige, for new programs, and for participation in graduate education, some difficult decisions will have to be made if the state is to avoid duplication of expensive services. No serious effort has yet been made to grapple with the problem of coordination.

Condensed from a report by
Professor Malcolm E. Jewell,
University of Kentucky,
March, 1968.

LOUISIANA   Although Louisiana has not built a system of higher education comparable in either size or quality to those of states such as Michigan or California, interest in higher education has been keen for the past 40 years. Probably most college-educated Louisianians have been educated in the state. Relatively few go outside the state for higher degrees and few non-Louisianians come in for them. Consequently, matters pertaining to higher education are of particular interest to Louisianians. A new faculty lounge in Baton Rouge, internecine quarreling in the Louisiana State University (LSU) department of political science, and student unrest at Grambling concerning alleged overemphasis on football—all are reported in the press and discussed widely.

To a large degree, however, this interest in higher education is not focused on academic matters. Scandals and sports are perhaps equal sources of interest. A winning football team at Louisiana State is seen as worth 100,000 votes. The Governor appears on television when a new coach is being signed, not infrequently has breakfast with high school students who are being recruited to a state college football team, and in general indicates his interest in the LSU athletic program.

Although much of the interest in higher education is not academic, it nevertheless has academic consequences. In all, 14 public institutions of higher education (including branches) have been established in Louisiana alongside approximately another 14 private institutions. Each small city and rural area desires its own college or university, despite the fact that there is not an area of the state well served by at least two B.A./B.S.—level institutions. Having a college or university in one's area is not only a source of income but also of prestige.

One of the major questions in Louisiana concerns the establishment of a system of junior colleges. Six of the state colleges established since the turn of the century began as two-year colleges. Gradually these institutions became regular four-year colleges, and some now grant graduate degrees as well. There is consequently apprehension that a new system of junior colleges would quickly go the same way.

Despite many arguments pro and con, the recent leveling off of enrollments and the recognition that a junior college system would be expensive will probably prevent one from being established. It also appears unlikely, for the same reasons, that the present number of colleges and universities will be expanded. The only difference in higher education in Louisiana over the next few decades will probably be a weakening of the private colleges and universities. Some, especially the small Negro colleges, may well disappear. By and large, the state system of higher education has been integrated, and the traditionally Negro public institutions have been expanded. Today a Negro in Louisiana can, for the most part, get a better education cheaper at a state college or university than at a private Negro school.

Another important issue concerns the direction that future improvements will take. Some argue that future resources should be channeled into enlarging existing facilities, not only in terms of physical plant but, more importantly, in terms of new schools (such as law and veterinary science) and the addition of graduate programs to institutions that have not had them in the past. The major argument made for such expansion is that Louisiana is presently unable to attract members of various professions (e.g., college teachers holding the Ph.D., primary and secondary teachers, physicians) and must consequently produce its own.

The other side of the argument is that these problems can best be solved by improving the quality of the present institutions, with perhaps specialization as to departments within the system. Such a policy would include improved salaries (LSU had in 1967 an average AAUP salary score of C, and the other state institutions had about a D score) and decreased teaching loads (which now vary from 12 to 15 hours in the state institutions). Of the two approaches, the second will probably win, although the outcome will be something of a compromise. There is a strong feeling in the state that college teachers lead a soft life, that there really is not much difference between one Ph.D. and the next, and that the people would be getting more for their money through more buildings, more teachers, and more degree programs and schools than by attracting a better faculty with higher salaries.

There are two major issues concerning the administrative organization of the state system. One concerns the alleged need of a coordinating board and the other, the role of the Legislature.

Presently, state higher education in Louisiana is run by two boards. Louisiana State University and its branches are administered by their own board, appointed by and large by the governor. This board has the largest influence in making education policy within the system. The LSU system consists of LSU (Baton Rouge) and three branches (another is planned). There is also the state board of education which is responsible not only for 10 state colleges and universities (including the traditionally Negro Southern University and its New Orleans branch and traditionally Negro Grambling College), but also for elementary and secondary education in Louisiana. Its members are elected.

In the spring session of 1969, the Legislature created a "superboard" to be appointed by the Governor. This board is not yet in operation, but it appears that its principal function will be coordination rather than the making of policy itself.

As indicated, the Legislature has little systematic authority over these powerful boards. Both boards must come to the Legislature for appropriations, but the Legislature only meets in regular sessions lasting 60 days in even-numbered years, and in odd-numbered years a fiscal session of 30 days is held. Major committees meet more frequently. On the whole, however, the Legislature, without staff, is at the mercy of the two boards when they bring requests. Both boards are composed to a significant degree of individuals with an independent political base who are generally able to get their own way.

There has been continual pressure on finances in Louisiana, as elsewhere. Probably due to the continued high returns from Louisiana's extractive industries combined with a slackening (perhaps even a leveling off) of enrollments, financial problems are not quite as severe here as they may be elsewhere. This year the tuition for Louisiana public colleges and universities was raised, despite considerable opposition. Although there is some variation in the system, tuition is in all cases below $300 a year. Louisiana has a strong Populist tradition, and the low tuition and universal admission policy of the state colleges and universities is very much a part of it.

In the next decade or two, no fundamental changes should be expected. In 1980 or so, the system will be slightly larger and have about the same composition. There will probably be a few more graduate departments in previously undergraduate colleges and the present universities may have a few new schools. There will probably also be the addition of five or so junior colleges, specializing in technical education. Racial integration will be well established throughout the system, excluding the two traditionally Negro institutions (Southern University and its New Orleans branch and Grambling College), which will remain predominantly Negro. In all probability, most of the better Negro students will attend the traditionally white colleges.

*Condensed from a report by
Professor Robert S. Robins,
Tulane University,
April, 1968.*

NEW YORK   The structure of higher education in New York is unique among the 50 states. A single administrative unit, the University of the State of New York, directed by a board of regents, has responsibility for all public and private higher education. The board of regents is also the governing instrument for elementary and secondary education. The commissioner of education serves also as president of the University of the State of New York. The board of regents is responsible for chartering all institutions of higher education, both public and private, in the state. The regents review all individual institutional plans.

The University of the State of New York is not to be confused with the State University of New York (SUNY). SUNY was founded in 1948, but for some time was little more than a loosely knit and minimally supported collection of state normal schools, agricultural and technical schools, and the contract colleges. Most observers agree that the development of SUNY was inhibited by vigorous opposition from the numerous and prestigious private institutions in New York. Following his election in 1958, Governor Rockefeller made the development of the public sector of the state's higher education a major part of his program.

SUNY is currently composed of 59 different campuses, including 31 community colleges (the latter supported one-third by local funds, one-third by state, and one-third by student fees). The state also pays half of the operating and capital costs of the City University of New York. In addition to direct institutional assistance through SUNY and CUNY, the state contributes to a system of student aid which includes various grants, loans, and fellowships.

One of the major questions facing policy makers is the extent and form that additional aid to the private sector should take. One hundred and forty-three private colleges and universities enroll a total of 233,000 students in the state. But direct institutional aid is barred by the so-called Blaine Amendment to the state constitution. The courts have interpreted the amendment as prohibiting any form of direct institutional assistance by the state to private educational institutions. In the fall of 1967 a substantial majority of the voters rejected a proposed new constitution which had as one of its most publicized aspects the repeal of the Blaine Amendment. In January, 1968, a gubernatorial commission recommended the repeal of the amendment and the provision of direct grants by the state to private institutions according to the number of degrees granted. The commission, chaired by Ford Foundation President McGeorge Bundy, also recommended considerably improved and increased central planning by the regents and the maintenance of quality standards as conditions of state aid. There is substantial disagreement over whether aid to private institutions should take the form recommended by the Bundy report or whether it should be in the form of increased scholarship and fellowship appropriations.

There are several arenas for consequential policy activity in New York higher education. Using the single phrase *higher education* to denote the multiplicity of institutions, functions, and administrative centers is itself a bit misleading. The agricultural and technical colleges, community colleges, state colleges, large private universities, the State University, and the City University involve more than a single dimension of public service and more than a single arena of policy conflict. Given this proliferation of centers of decision making, major policies tend to be made in response to dramatic stimuli which temporarily overwhelm potential opposition. The recent expansion of SUNY, with the careful and extensive support structure created at the behest of Governor Rockefeller, is an instance of such a stimulus.

It is possible to identify at least four centers of initiative within New York higher education, two of which find the governor playing a central role. First, in terms of the budgetary process and the program planning which can be stimulated through it, there are the director of the budget and the governor. The Division of the Budget seems to have served more as a central planning agency than as a "pruner and picker," at least in matters affecting higher education. The New York budget office is one of the country's most highly professionalized. Eight to ten budget officers devote full time to higher educational matters. This compares with one member of the staff of the Assembly Ways and Means Committee who handles higher education along with seven other functions.

The trustees of SUNY present an integrated budget to the Division of the Budget, which in turn incorporates it as seen fit by the governor into the executive budget. CUNY requests are integrated as part of the local assistance requests forwarded by the Mayor of New York City to the Division of the Budget. Again, the latter serves as nearly the sole channel for formal communication with the legislative committees. Appropriation requests from the contract colleges are technically submitted as part of the SUNY budget; however, there has been inadequate experience with this procedure to allow evaluation. It is a potential focal point of continued controversy.

The second center of policy initiative in higher education is within the Department of Education, particularly in the person of Dr. Allen and his deputy for matters of higher education, Ewald Nyquist. The commissioner is appointed by the regents. Instances of conflict between the Governor and the Department of Education are not uncommon, although seldom visible to the public. There seems to be some remnants of jealousy within the department toward the growth of SUNY. Due to his strong identification with SUNY, Rockefeller is evidently one of the specific objects of this antagonism. Most observers find it difficult to separate the role of the Governor from the policies of SUNY as articulated by Chancellor Samuel B. Gould, who represents a third principal policy maker. He was the personal choice of Governor Rockefeller in 1964, and his directorship of the recent growth of SUNY is evidently much to Rockefeller's liking. However, faced with the necessity of requesting substantial tax increases, the Governor made considerable cuts in the requests from SUNY for 1968-69. This was the first instance of potentially serious conflict between the Governor and the chancellor.

The fourth arena of higher educational policy is not so much a central part of the state machinery as it is a residual constituency. This is the melange of private institutions in the state. Five private universities and a multitude of denominational and unaffiliated colleges still enroll over half of the students in New York higher education. But their effectiveness as voices for specific policy initiation is somewhat limited by their diverse nature and loose ties to the state. Relative to SUNY and CUNY, the large private universities are less oriented to the specific needs of New York than they are to regional or national clienteles.

Due in large part to a minimal commitment by the state until recent years, New York has expanded its commitment of public resources for higher education at a rate probably matched by few other states. The initiative in forming higher educational policy has rested almost exclusively with the Governor, the State and City Universities, and with the Department of Education. The Legislature's role is entirely one of review and occasional amendment. Although there has been some leveling off in the rate of enrollment increase, the universal expectation is that the state's commitment to higher education must continue to be expanded. At the present time, the particular concern is with how, not whether, the state can increase its support to the private institutions. The traditional antipathy between the private institutions and those in the public sector seems to have subsided considerably in recent years. The likelihood that some contrary purposes occasionally will continue to be articulated in the policy-making arenas, however, is quite high. Furthermore, many state leaders will admit that some of the large private institutions may soon be absorbed entirely into the state system.

Nearly all members of the Legislature, regardless of party, express approval of the growth that has taken place in recent years. Although they are concerned about the financial problems, they expect to continue their support to meet continuing demands. Some dissatisfaction exists with central planning performed by the regents, but not such that it would be likely to cause negative reactions to budget requests. The willingness to "let the professionals do their job" minimizes the necessity for legislators to expand their own expertise in matters of higher education.

Despite the magnitude of appropriations, few legislators have clearly formulated priorities in their own minds as to the various purposes served by higher education. They have no specific conception of the nature or amount of federal aid currently going to the state's institutions of higher education. No major private interest groups are active exclusively in the area of higher education. This may be due to the specialization which characterizes higher education policy. But it is also probably due to the low salience of the Legislature as a consequential arena for policy making. Expansion of higher educational opportunities is seen as a wise investment in the economic development of the state. Most politicians, without apparent complacency, feel that New York is meeting its needs in higher education as well as, and probably better than, most other states.

Condensed from a report by
Professor Richard I. Hofferbert,
Cornell University,
April, 1968.

PENNSYLVANIA The major issues in Pennsylvania revolve around the question of how to meet the increasing demand for public higher education.

Although unanimously proud of Pennsylvania's colleges and universities, many of the legislators we interviewed indicated that the state's education budget was inadequate and not being spent as efficiently and effectively as it could be. Greater statewide coordination and control of higher educational planning and appropriations seems to be sorely needed.

The financial squeeze is considerable. Educational costs are rising, and state colleges are overcrowded and swamped with many more applications than they can accommodate. Current state resources are inadequate to meet the state's higher educational needs. In 1966 Pennsylvania budgeted over $95 million to higher education. Compared on a per capita basis with other states in the nation, this was not outstanding. At $8.20 per head, Pennsylvania spent less than half what the average state allocated to higher education and ranked 48 among the 50 states.

Pennsylvania legislators anticipated difficulty in getting additional funds for higher education. In their opinion, the increasing public demand for higher education is not matched by increasing public willingness to foot the bill for expanding educational facilities. Pennsylvanians are extremely resistant to any increase in taxes.

Coordinating the programs of the state's 140 institutions of higher education is a primary concern. In the past there has been little communication and less coordination among private schools and between public and private colleges and universities. Public initiative and guidance of higher education, both legislative and executive, have been weak.

It is probably proper to describe past public coordination of the 14 state-owned colleges, 16 state-supported private schools, the fledgling community college system, and the remaining institutions—most of them private—as minimal. Although responsibility for approving all curriculum and facilities planning for the 14 state-owned institutions is centered in the state Department of Public Instruction, the private schools, which play the major role in higher education in the state, develop academic and facilities plans independently. Their programs are coordinated neither among themselves nor with the public institutions. At present, all Pennsylvania's 140 institutions, public as well as private, are administered independently by autonomous governing boards.

Greater statewide coordination and control—particularly of college and university budget requests—is essential. Currently, all schools which receive state funds submit annual requests to a central body, the state board of education. But the requests are not integrated or reviewed as a whole. There is some coordination of state college and community college requests, but the Pennsylvania Legislature receives no single, integrated budget for the entire system. Individual institutions present their requests separately. The result is much brisk lobbying by representatives of individual schools. Such a system, or lack of system, makes it easier for the private institutions, which have powerful legislative liaison, to perpetuate their status as liberally subsidized institutions almost wholly autonomous of effective state regulation.

The dual issue of state support and state regulation of the private institutions is becoming increasingly salient to Pennsylvania legislators. Pennsylvania has many private schools, but no large system of *public* higher education. Of 140 institutions, only 14 are strictly state-owned and -governed. The state does not even have a major public university. Pennsylvania State, usually considered the state's university, is partly a private corporation, not under state control. (Less than one-third of its governing board is publicly elected or appointed. This stands in contrast to most states, where state-financed university boards are dominated by public representatives). Traditionally, and currently, private colleges and universities serve, as one state senator put it, as "the backbone of higher education" in Pennsylvania.

The major trouble with the current system is that neither the state-owned nor the private, state-supported institutions are accommodating the increasing demand of Pennsylvanians for higher education. In spite of increased appropriations to state colleges and a crash building program, there simply are not enough facilities in the 14 state-owned colleges to admit all the qualified applicants. They often turn away thousands of students, including many in the top half of their high school graduating classes. With the number of applicants rising each year, the pressure on the state colleges is not expected to diminish.

While the state-owned colleges turn away qualified students, many state-subsidized private schools have vacancies which go unfilled. Allowed almost total autonomy in the expenditure of the state money they receive, and free to set their own admissions standards and curriculum policies, the private schools have failed, in the view of some state leaders, to satisfactorily serve the best educational interests of the people of the state. Specifically, they complain that Pennsylvania's colleges and universities have become too exclusive—both financially and scholastically—and that they are catering too much to the best students and to the affluent.

Pressured by parents and would-be students, Pennsylvania is seeking to develop a statewide system of higher education which will adequately and efficiently serve the people of the state. The most essential step is to require that state-subsidized private institutions, such as the University of Pennsylvania in Philadelphia, accept public regulation in return for state support.

Although a few of the legislators with whom we talked approved of this idea, others indicated reluctance to attach any strings to the money which the private schools receive from the state. Lack of legislative consensus on this issue was reflected in the comments of two state assemblymen. The first affirmed that the state "will have to take a more active role in directing the private colleges." The second declared, with equal conviction, that the state should by no means "impose any admissions or curriculum controls" on the public schools.

Several factors will make state control of the private institutions difficult to achieve. Above all, there is considerable pride in Pennsylvania's tradition of private higher education—a widespread attitude that the private schools are somehow better than the public and that it would be improper for the state to demand a dominant voice in the administration of private recipients of public funds. Other factors include strong support of the autonomous status of the private schools from metropolitan interests and from alumni-legislators and skillful lobbying by administrative officials of the various private schools.

To date, efforts to develop a more efficient, coordinated system of higher education in Pennsylvania have met with limited success. A master plan for state higher education, prepared under a 1963 mandate from the General Assembly, was completed by the state board of education in the fall of 1966. However, at the time of this report, only three of the board's recommendations had been implemented. They were (1) creation of a liaison committee of the state Board for Private Institutions, (2) reorganization of the Department of Public Instruction, and (3) expansion of the state's program of student scholarships.

Pennsylvania legislators expressed considerable consternation over the General Assembly's failure to make much progress in passing legislation to enact the master plan. Said one: "A lot of legislation has been drafted . . . but it gets no place . . . [we] haven't had committee hearings on it. It's a disgrace, really." The difficulty seems to be not merely legislative inertia. The only time Pennsylvania's private colleges and universities have coordinated their efforts has been in opposition to the provisions of the master plan.

In addition, two issues were frequently mentioned by respondents: (1) the need to correct an overemphasis on broad, liberal arts education and to develop more vocational-technical and professional training programs and (2) the need to revise the state scholarship program.

There seems to be general agreement that Pennsylvania schools — public and private — have placed too much emphasis on providing broad, liberal arts education and have neglected vocational-technical training. Almost every legislator interviewed mentioned that Pennsylvania needed more medical schools and had not sufficiently developed programs for graduate and professional training of other kinds. Many suggested that the system was not producing enough people with socially valuable, marketable skills, and thus was not providing the kind of stimulus to the state's economy that it should.

There also appears to be a strong feeling among legislators that the state scholarship program, administered by the recently created Higher Education Assistance Agency, should be reviewed and revised. Specifically, they maintained that, in the last three years, the scholarship program has expanded too rapidly and been administered too liberally — not only that it is extraordinarily expensive, but that it is furnishing scholarship money to students who do not need it, or who could, with help from their families, pay a much larger portion of their own college expenses.

Prepared by Jean Harrison,
June, 1969.

TEXAS The character of Texas politics has left a deep imprint on higher education and will continue to do so. In the 1930s and 1940s, higher education was very much a part of the Texas political system, in the rough-and-tumble fashion of the politics of the day. Higher education in Texas today is much less political. It has attained power over the past decade and has won a new acceptability, rather than, at best, a grudging tolerance. This is not to claim that Texas political leaders will no longer intervene in the internal life of Texas colleges and universities. However, higher education has its supporters, not only in fiscal matters but in the attainment of academic quality.

Currently, Texas supports 22 senior colleges and universities, 3 medical colleges (in Galveston, Dallas, and San Antonio), 31 junior colleges, and several technical and scientific institutions. Texas has never seen substantial development, either in quantitative or qualitative terms, of its private colleges. Public institutions of higher learning enroll 80 percent of students beyond high school. Enrollment increases are taking place almost exclusively in the public schools. Only three private schools enroll as many as 6,000 students, a figure exceeded by 13 of the 22 state-supported schools. There are two exceptions to the generalizations about the relative lack of quality and quantity in the private schools. Rice University, a privately endowed institution in Houston, is in some scientific and technical fields recognized as superior. And Baylor University's medical college in Houston currently graduates about one-third of all Texas M.D.'s and probably produces as high a quality of graduate as do the public medical schools.

What should be emphasized about the private schools is their relatively low saliency in Texas political decision making. There has been little coordination in the past between private and public schools, although the Coordinating Board is taking halting steps in that direction. Nor has there been much competition between the two.

In contrast to private schools, junior colleges are extremely important in political decision making with respect to higher education. The state has 31 public junior colleges and 20 private junior colleges, most of the latter being small and strongly church-related. As a part of Governor Connally's educational reorganization, administration of junior colleges (to the degree that the state does administer them) was given to the Coordinating Board, Texas College and University System (the so-called superboard). Funds for the junior colleges come mostly from local taxation and student charges, but about a third of their income is derived from state sources.

Junior colleges are designed to provide both a terminal education and to serve as "feeder" institutions for four-year colleges. Some observers have doubted that Texas junior colleges have performed either function very well, which probably reflects both their inadequate financial base and their local control. There apparently is no movement underway to provide more state direction for the junior colleges although, if legislative attitudes are any guide to policy, Texas will see a massive growth in state assistance to the junior colleges.

The politics of higher education is changing as the newly created Coordinating Board develops political resources and as the board and the Legislature begin to develop rules, roles, and expectations about each other's behavior. The Coordinating Board is a product of Governor Connally's swelling education reforms, the impetus for which was provided by his Committee on Education Beyond the High School, created at his request by the Legislature in 1963. The committee recommended major reforms in higher educational structure and finance.

Despite a characteristic elephantine slowness in responding to major reforms, the Legislature responded quickly to the Governor's recommendations for a Coordinating Board. The board, created in 1965, was empowered to perform a variety of planning, administrative, and review functions. In addition to these responsibilities, the board also serves as a staff agency to both the governor and to the Legislature. One important role in this context is its charge to render opinions to the Legislature on any bill which would add a unit to the state system or which would change the status of any existing unit.

A second staff responsibility of the board is to develop formulas for financing components of higher education and to advise both the governor's budget office and the Legislative Budget Board regarding institutional requests for funds.

Governor Connally made educational improvement a major tenet of his legislative program and the Legislature has followed his lead in this area. The notion of strong central coordination of higher education was particularly appealing to the major universities and to their legislators, since it could be utilized to oppose the proposals of small schools wanting to offer complete programs and graduate degrees in every field of scholarly endeavor.

The strength of the Governor of Texas in politics is enhanced by the relative complexity of the legislative process, by the short biennial session of the Legislature, and by the relatively high turnover in the Legislature. Customarily, even the speakership changes hands each session, although the present incumbent has occupied it for two terms.

An understanding of the legislative powers of the governor and the speaker is fundamental to understanding the politics of higher education, since both Governor Connally and Speaker Barnes have proven to be powerful supporters of increased appropriations and reorganization of higher education.

The most powerful legislators appear to be members of the Budget Board, composed of four members of each house, the speaker, and the lieutenant governor. The board writes the legislative budget and is thus a kind of super-appropriations committee. The power of board members is further strengthened by the fact that they are likely to be leaders of the respective money committees and members of the conference committee on appropriations. It would be difficult to imagine a single group of legislators who enjoy more formal power in a legislative body. The Budget Board controls appropriations with an iron hand.

In the context of the conservative coloration of Texas politics over the past decade, higher education has fared rather well, at least in a fiscal sense. The situation could change abruptly, however, if the balance of power within the Democratic party or between the Democratic and Republican parties were to shift—or if a less supportive governor were to be elected. It may seem odd to attribute so much power to a governor whose formal powers are relatively limited. Nonetheless, the progress of higher education in the past decade, or half-decade, has depended to a large degree on the incumbent governor. Perhaps in California there are enough other liberalizing influences to enable higher education to weather the storm of an archconservative, but this is not the case in Texas, where a governor who is not oriented to higher education and its problems could bring progress to a screeching halt.

Condensed from a report by
Professor Robert L. Lineberry,
University of Texas,
May, 1968.

2. Prospects and Problems

The American states vary markedly in economic development, social and ethnic stratification, political structure and culture, administrative organization, and popular attitudes toward a variety of matters—from the secular and profane to the religious and sacred.

Such differences are reflected in the goals which these states set for higher education and in their ability to achieve them. Higher education is, quite clearly, expected to fulfill diverse and sometimes conflicting functions. Among the most common of these are an education in the arts and humanities, the provision of opportunities for low-income and minority groups, training in vocational skills, the supplying of persons with professional and scientific competence, and the transmission of societal beliefs and values. The emphasis placed upon these goals is likely to vary from state to state according to the characteristics of the states' populations, their unique social and economic problems, and the expectations that leaders and citizens entertain concerning them.

States with unfavorable political environments, little executive or administrative talent, or small tax bases are likely to find it difficult to achieve many of their educational ends. Even with the best of intentions, not all states are able to overcome their economic and political handicaps. Also the organization of a state educational system is likely to influence capabilities in higher education. A state without some type of centralized coordinating body may not be able to utilize its resources efficiently or effectively; a state with a politically controlled governing board may not be able to shield its universities from partisan conflict.

An additional factor is the idiosyncratic influence of personality. In a number of the states in the survey—New York, Texas, and Iowa, for example—an energetic and capable governor was credited with large-scale innovations and improvements in higher education; in at least one other state, a governor had emerged who was trying to reduce the university's budget and influence. Thus individual leadership can be as much of a factor in the states' successes in higher education as their social, economic, or political "givens."

It should be pointed out that in most of the subsequent chapters the respondents' perceptions will not be linked with the particular conditions and institutional arrangements of their respective states. What justifies this procedure, as many excerpts from the interviews will show, is that state legislators and other officials respond to general questions in general terms and that their responses, though conditioned by the particular state environment, are by no means exclusively "state-bound." Within-state responses are likely to be as heterogeneous as between-state responses; so that, if one did not know a particular respondent's locale, one would be hard put to guess it from his answers. While states differ greatly from each other, within-state differences are also considerable. As a result, a Texas Democrat's responses may resemble those of a Pennsylvania Republican, or an urban legislator's responses in Kansas may resemble those made by a New York rural official, or a Californian's conservative answers may be much like those of a Louisiana liberal. A state's particular socioeconomic, cultural, or political configuration affects, but by no means determines, response patterns. And insofar as these configurations are not unique, the profile of perceptions and attitudes that emerges from all respondents' answers can well be considered that of "a nation of states."

An appropriate opening for a report like this is to present some of the most general perceptions, attitudes, and appraisals. How do legislators and executives feel about the development of higher education in their states? How do they evaluate their educational systems? How do they compare their own system with those in other states? What do they see as the major problems facing higher education? Our first two questions were highly unstructured, simply asking: "How do you feel things in higher education have been going in (state) over the past few years?" and "As you see it, what are some of the major problems?"

GENERAL SATISFACTION WITH HIGHER EDUCATION　It appeared that the state officials were, with a few exceptions, pleased. Most respondents indicated that "things" had been proceeding well in their states and compared their own state's educational system favorably with those in other states.

However, certain differentiating patterns in state responses were apparent. Officials from the smaller, less wealthy states seemed more contented with their public colleges and universities — despite the admitted superiority of higher education in the larger, more wealthy states. Respondents from California and New York, paradoxically, recognized their own leadership in higher education but were generally less optimistic about the situation and saw greater problems in the future. Thus, although these latter states had made great strides in education, they had apparently encountered major difficulties in developing and managing the enterprise. Respondents in New York and California suggested that the problems of recent years might outweigh the gains.

GENERAL APPRAISAL Positive appraisals of "things in higher education" typically were expressed in terms of increased appropriations. A Texas legislator, for example, replied, "Things have been going well financially." One of his colleagues volunteered: "Well, in the last four years, the state appropriations have doubled. So I would say that we are making very forward steps toward progress." Most Texans seemed to feel that higher education had been doing exceptionally well in the past five years and that, as one respondent put it, Texas "is now in a position to develop a higher educational system second to none in the nation." An Assemblyman said: "The expenditures have gone up some 200 percent in the state of Texas over the last few years. . . . We certainly recognize that education is the solution to many, many problems."

Legislators in Kentucky, Illinois, Iowa, and Kansas generally offered similar comments. Improvements in educational quality, physical facilities, and faculty salaries were cited. A Kansas respondent felt that his state's universities were among the best in the nation:

I think here in Kansas we have progress in higher education. Certainly our universities are among the best in the nation, especially the University of Kansas. Kansas State also is a fine university, and Wichita is becoming quite good, and I feel that our colleges are good. We are giving them what I consider to be quite good budgetary support. I feel that our situation concerning education in Kansas, including the junior colleges, is quite good.

An Iowa legislator said:

Well, I think there's been a great improvement in physical facilities as well as salary scale. I recall down through the years that . . . the regents were setting their sights at the upping of the salary scale to about third place in the 10 or 11 comparable institutions in the Midwest, and I think we've reached that. In fact, at one point, I think we were near second. . . . I would say the . . . Legislature has made some giant steps in bringing us up to date in this area.

The California and New York leaders tended to be less positive. Asked, "How are things going?" a New York legislator replied:

Not good, not good at all! All education in New York has seemed to be dealt with not as it should be. I think there ought to be a greater attack on the problems of higher education than we have made in the past several years. I wouldn't say that we have been standing still — we have done a lot. But what we've done is not any way near what we should be doing, and it is only picking up some of the things which had not been done for a number of years before then.

A California legislator said:

There's been a reduction in financial support and . . . we've noticed the expression of an attitude which is, I wouldn't say anti-intellectual, but certainly not sympathetic with the problems of the University or the role of the University or the role of the faculty. . . . And I think if you don't have the proper appreciation of its role or its function, then you're liable to pursue policies which would be adverse to its interests.

Another Californian thought that the time had come for a complete reevaluation of the state's system of higher education:

We've had a lot of problems in higher education. . . . I think . . . we've got to sit down and reevaluate our whole system of higher education in California. I think there [are] some basic flaws in the relationships that we have between the University system and the state college and our junior college program. And the Master Plan for Higher Education needs to be overhauled.

COMPARISON WITH OTHER STATES
Most leaders felt that their states compared favorably with others in higher education and expected that they would continue to do so. Their acclamations ranged from the semiautomatic "We are just doing fine" to the boastful "State University is as good as any other in the country."

In making comparisons, most respondents tended to adopt criteria which allowed them to view their state's educational system favorably. A Texas leader, for example, declared that his state was "at the bottom of the upper one-third." Legislators from California and New York often made comparisons with each other's educational systems. Although respondents from other states also cited California and New York schools as yardsticks for their own systems, most tended to make comparisons with states which were similar in the level of educational development or economic wealth or were of geographic proximity. Many different criteria were used to show that a state was "doing well" relative to others.

While most state politicians were pleased with their own colleges and universities, it was clear that many regarded California and New York as the leaders. The consensus of New York respondents seemed to be that the schools were rapidly catching up to those in California. They were pleased with the development. "Yes, we make that comparison with California all the time," said one official. "During the whole debate in the early sixties, the question of California and New York always came up. . . . I think we are keeping up with them. We weren't for a long time, but we are now." A colleague concurred:

The general concept is that there are no other states [except] California that are doing a better job than we are. . . . I'm not sure but that we are even with them now. But certainly in their junior college program they are a bit beyond what we've got.

A number of California respondents agreed that their state was losing ground to New York. Typical of several remarks:

I think we're number one, but New York is catching up with us. In the next five years we will be number two. . . . At the rate we're going, we will not be able to keep up. We're going to have to be cutting back. Instead of talking about growing in California with population demands, we are talking about backpedaling.

Officials in the other wealthy states surveyed—Illinois, Texas, and Pennsylvania—also drew comparisons with New York and California on occasion. They generally recognized the superiority of the schools there. An Illinois administrator, for example, said his state compared itself with California, not with national norms. "I think that Illinois has one of the better educational systems in the country," he added. A Texas legislator also compared his state's accomplishments with those of California. "They are way ahead of us," he admitted, "but I would say that in 10 years we can have a program here to compare."

Respondents from the less wealthy states generally compared their schools with those in states of similar economic resources or with those in neighboring states. Several respondents from Kentucky thought that their state was doing all right, considering that it was one of the poorer. A Senator commented:

Now, from my knowledge of what exists in other states and Kentucky, I don't know of any area that we're lagging behind in higher education. Oh, true, we could pick out some states with heavily endowed colleges and that sort of thing, and some states with heavier taxes, such as California, that are perhaps doing more than Kentucky as far as ability to pay goes. . . . Certainly for a state like Kentucky, not the richest of the states by any means, we're making, I think, maximum effort in higher education.

Another Kentuckian remarked:

I think, at least in comparison with the surrounding states, I think we are keeping up — giving a good account of ourselves . . . even Ohio, which is a lot richer state. I think we are doing as good a job as they are. And I'm certain with West Virginia and Tennessee, the states at about the same economic level with us, that we're doing a better job.

A Kansas Senator compared his state favorably with others in the region, and a Texas legislator said:

I'm highly pleased. At least so far as with what we would classify as the Southern states or the Southwestern states are concerned. Having served on the Southern Regional Education Board which includes 16 states, except for perhaps Florida and Maryland, I would say that we rank number one.

Among those who mentioned specific bases of comparison, the criteria were mixed. An Iowa leader expressed pride in the University of Iowa and declared, "What really makes that institution great is . . . the caliber of people that are there teaching and the caliber of the students." Another Iowan mentioned educational innovations as well as high-caliber graduates:

I think Iowa has been very, very competitive in the higher educational field. I think we've shown several innovations — the area school system being one of them. The University of Iowa is recognized across the nation. . . . We've produced many people of high caliber in this state who've been national leaders in scientific, in literary fields.

A Kansas Senator also pointed to the high quality of his state's university graduates:

At Kansas University, for example, we are given information that for state universities in the Midwest and the whole country, we turn out more Woodrow Wilson Fellows and Rhodes Scholars and so on—indicating an academic excellence in our university that exceeds almost all state schools.

A member of the Texas House based his pride on progress in the number of Ph.D.'s being produced: "We are perhaps behind the top one or two in production of Ph.D.'s, but I think that we will catch up in that because of the enhancement of funding in the last six to eight years, and it will compare favorably with any of the other states."

But not all respondents expressed approval of their state's progress. A Texas Assemblyman, for instance, thought that his state had only one good school:

You have to talk about higher education in Texas in two completely different frames of reference—one is the University of Texas at Austin and the other is everybody else. If you talk about Austin, I think you would have to say that we are up with the top 10 or 15 public institutions in the country. Perhaps I am overoptimistic about that, but I get the impression that we are making some very important strides at that institution. If you talk about the rest of them, I think that they are sadly substandard. If you compare them with California, it is just ludicrous. If you compare them with the State University system in New York, it is just . . . well, there is not any comparison. . . . The basic problem here is that we have too many schools, too little central coordination, and too much politics involved in who gets what.

A California Assemblyman felt that his state was "good but not as good as we've been led to believe as it relates to the other schools. We think of ourselves as having an outstanding higher educational system, but it's really not—it doesn't quite stack up when you start true measurement of it with other states."

Several Pennsylvania legislators mentioned that their state did not have a large public educational system, but rather a great many private schools. It was difficult, then, they maintained, for their public schools to compete with Western states, which had extensive public educational systems. One Pennsylvanian explained:

I think we have a good higher educational system in Pennsylvania. As stated before, one of our problems has been that we do not have a large public educational system. . . . Now you go out West, you'll find that there's greater emphasis on the public education because when the colonists, the early settlers, moved West . . . the churches did not build the colleges such as they've built in Pennsylvania. So in the Western states, the state governments took the responsibility of constructing public colleges and universities. Now our problem has been to take the present private and public education system in Pennsylvania and devise a system that will adequately serve the people of the state. This hasn't been easy.

MAJOR PROBLEMS IN HIGHER EDUCATION

While the majority of state officials were satisfied with their state's progress in higher education, most also felt that serious problems remained unsolved. The pattern of response from state to state was fairly consistent in this respect. The most frequently mentioned problems were financing, planning and coordination, enrollment increases, and student unrest. Each of these topics was covered at a later point in the questionnaire and will be considered in subsequent chapters.

Less often mentioned was concern over such matters as legislative attitudes toward academicians and the public service role of higher education. These elicited interesting comments, however, which will be reported in separate chapters.

3. *Information and Pressures*

Our survey showed that legislators face serious dilemmas in legislating for and funding higher education. Although called upon to allocate millions of dollars for state colleges and universities, they are severely constrained by lack of relevant information—and in many cases, not so much by the sheer absence of knowledge as by its incompleteness or inaccuracy and by the conditions under which legislators must work.

Paradoxically, these malfunctions of the information system are built into the legislative process. Despite protestations to the contrary, the legislator himself is the source of his informational troubles. It is said, sometimes, that the politician hears with a "third ear," but this third ear can be and often is a deceptive device. It hears what it wants to hear; it selects, screens, distorts, and omits. It cannot do otherwise; the constraints of the representational process make it so.

For that matter, even the most accurate, reliable, and complete information is not ipso facto conducive to the making of sound judgments about the broad range of issues that confront the modern legislator. The great variety and complexity of the issues, the time pressures that inexorably call for action, or the need to respond to political demands regardless of their soundness make utilization of information, even when available, extremely difficult. This is not to say that the legislator should not have at his disposal as full information as possible when and if he wants or needs it. And for this reason alone an efficient information system should be available to the legislative body as an institution. But, precisely because the legislative process in all its complexity generates its own constraints, no legislator can inform himself fully on all the issues which he is called upon to decide. His task would be insuperable.

Moreover, the very nature of the representational task makes for "noise" in the legislative channels of communication. It is the great virtue of the broadly based representative body that it can respond collectively to a variety of societal needs precisely because each of its individual members can and will respond selectively to those demands that come to his focus of attention. From this perspective, limited information, one-sided information, or perhaps even no information at all is as crucial to the performance of the representational function as is full and accurate information. The legislature's task, after all, is not to determine Truth but to reconcile conflicting interests.

The legislator, then, is not simply the passive recipient of information that he somehow uses to his best lights as he represents interests and makes decisions. Rather, he is himself an important purveyor of information in the legislature's total informational system. He brings to public attention and to the attention of his colleagues what he thinks is in the interest of his own goals or the goals of those for whom he speaks. It may be in his interest or his clientele's interest to reveal information as much as to conceal it. To ask of every legislator that he be well informed on all matters on which he must decide is to ask not only the impossible but probably the undesirable. If he often listens only with the third ear and keeps his other two ears shut, it is because he may have to cut himself off from information or at least make it so usable for his own purposes that he can reach or accept a decision with which he can live.

FACTORS AFFECTING THE FLOW OF INFORMATION A state legislator's major, and sometimes exclusive, role in making higher educational policy seems to be that of voting, or not voting, on appropriations for the state colleges and universities. Requests and information reaching him from institutions of higher learning deal almost solely with budgetary matters. Differences in the extent to which information is channeled to individual legislators and the kind of information coming to them seem to be largely due to four factors: first, the degree to which the legislature serves as the effective decision-making body for appropriations to higher education; second, the legislator's formal position in the legislature; third, whether or not his district contains a state-supported college or university; and fourth, the legislator's personal involvement in the problems of higher education.

THE
EFFECTIVE
LOCUS OF
DECISION
MAKING
Formally, of course, all legislatures control the purse strings of higher education, but they vary considerably in the extent to which they are the effective centers of decision. And this variation, in turn, is reflected in legislators' levels of information. We can illustrate this by pointing to the stark contrast between New York and Pennsylvania. In New York, the Legislature, by the admission of our respondents, acts as a reviewing and amending body only. New York legislators reported receiving almost no direct appeals for appropriations from individual colleges or universities. A Ways and Means Committee member, asked how the needs of higher education came to his attention,* freely conceded: "I'm not well informed, to be honest with you. The regents do the planning." Another New Yorker, asked how the claims of various institutions reached the Legislature, reported that he was never contacted by educational lobbyists: "Our orbits just don't cross. They don't know me, and I don't know them."

But the Pennsylvania Legislature plays a central and effective role in appropriations for higher education. Pennsylvania respondents reported that they frequently received direct requests for funding from individual institutions. According to a member of the Senate, "Most of the requests I receive come directly from the university officials." A member of the Pennsylvania House was specific:

Most of the schools, Penn State, Temple, University of Pennsylvania, Drexel, all have liaison men to the Legislature. In effect, lobbyists. They're in daily communication with the legislative leaders as to their budget and their financial needs. When the situation becomes quite urgent, as it did in late 1967, when we were in an impasse in the state over a tax battle . . . the presidents of these institutions themselves journeyed down to Harrisburg and met with the Democratic . . . and Republican leaders. So there is no lack of communication between the schools and the legislative leaders.

THE
LEGISLATOR'S
FORMAL
POSITION
In states where the legislature plays a key role in setting appropriations for higher education, both formal and informal requests from individual campuses tend to be channeled to the individuals

*The questions used to elicit responses on this subject: "I suppose that many colleges and universities make requests to you here in the Legislature. How are these requests brought to your attention? Are you generally satisfied or not satisfied with the way the needs of higher education are handled and brought to you?"

who occupy the crucial gate-keeping positions in the legislative hierarchy—particulary chairmen and senior members of committees or subcommittees dealing with taxes and appropriations. Moreover, the flow of information seems to cease at this point in the decision-making process. Rank-and-file members remain uninformed and, by implication, must accept the recommendations of those in a position to know.

A California leader said:

Let me put it this way. I'm now a senior member of the Senate. I'm now in the upper quarter of the men here on the basis of seniority, so I'm put into committees where the needs become more obvious to me. But to the men who are not, I think they have real voids [in information]. The men who have never served on the Education or Finance Committees—that's the majority of the Senate—I don't think they know enough about it. I don't think it's brought to them enough.

A Kansas legislator, asked about the system of budgetary procedure in his state, made a similar comment. How respondents outside the privileged circle of key committee members experience the constraints placed on information by the legislative structure was explained by another Kansan: "Very seldom do people talk to me. I am not on the Ways and Means Committee. People know the structure, so they don't talk to me."

SCHOOL IN
DISTRICT

It stands to reason that legislators from districts where state-supported colleges or universities are located would hear more about problems of higher education and would be more likely to receive direct requests than other legislators. A few illustrations must suffice. A Texas leader with a junior college in his district reported:

I have a lot of contact with junior college people. They are much more active in talking about their appropriations and seeking help. Of course, I have no senior colleges in my district—no state-supported senior colleges. This could be the reason for it.

A Kansan whose district included a state university told us:

I am from Wichita, and I do get more individual pressure. The university, for example, had some of us legislators to dinner . . . and they talked to us about their needs. . . . I also get telephone calls or letters from individual administrators and faculty or department heads, and even students—usually on specific issues.

Another legislator with a university in his home town indicated he received more information than most of his colleagues.

PERSONAL
INVOLVEMENT

Finally, some respondents indicated that the extent to which they received information or requests directed to them individually was largely due to their own interests in and involvement with educators and their problems. A California legislator reported that most of his information came from "friends in higher education," and that he had "many friends who are in some way connected with the campus."

My campaign manager just finished his doctoral dissertation . . . and is an instructor in political science. My finance chairman is a professor. . . . I spend a great deal of time with faculty people.

A Kansas respondent explained why he was more frequently contacted than most of his colleagues:

Well, I suppose because I have been associated with it for so many years, I have established a pretty well-defined pattern of liaison and communication with college heads. I visit the campuses, and I am well acquainted with the heads of the schools and their fiscal officers and the board of regents and its fiscal officers.

SATISFACTION
WITH THE
FLOW OF
INFORMATION

State legislators' comments on their satisfactions or dissatisfactions with the ways in which the needs of higher education were brought to their attention revealed an interesting dilemma. On the one hand, a pervasive theme was a desire for more information. Many respondents felt that they were not sufficiently advised about the plans, programs, and expenditures of state-supported institutions. On the other hand, the leaders and key committee members with whom we talked complained about being terribly pressed for time and their inability to absorb all of the information that reached them. A seat in the legislature is generally a part-time job. Legislative hearings on higher education are typically short and are often held biennially rather than annually. Other commitments in other areas of legislative work make it almost impossible for the average legislator to study and digest the kind of detailed information on higher education that is in fact available.

A desire to know more about specific programs and expenditures of state-supported colleges and universities was voiced by many legislators. A New York leader expressed his dissatisfaction with the "generalities" presented by witnesses from educational institutions in budgetary hearings:

I must say . . . at times it is almost impossible for a legislator to understand what these educators are saying. We get . . . such generalities in the budget hearings. I just say to myself, "Now Sam, what do you do about this?" If you have the time and the will, I suppose you can find out. . . . The problem is that there is so much to be done, that it is impossible for a legislator to cover everything.

A California Assemblyman wished that the legislators were presented more specific information, "so that we can figure out how much it costs for a specific thing. We can't find that out." A member of the Iowa House Committee on Higher Education elaborated on this point. Asked if he was satisfied with the way requests were presented to the Legislature, he replied:

No, I can't say that I am. The Legislature, to accomplish its work in a short period of time, deals with generalities too much. We're not specific enough . . . particularly in higher education. I don't think we as legislators are particularly aware of the problems of the university or private colleges. Very few of the legislators have gone into the business office of a college or university and explored the books and found out exactly what are the financial problems, or talked to the dean of students, for example, to see what types of problems they have in student relationships. We hear many times specific instances which are brought up stressing specific points. But I don't think that we have enough information to make solid, rational decisions.

A member of the Kentucky House Appropriations Committee was emphatic in his criticism:

The system in Kentucky is so damn backwards and mixed up. . . . How can you, with these budget figures, know something about the programs? You don't need to know all the details, but I think we need to know something about the programs being proposed. We need to know why these programs are being developed and why they need the money. . . . I think we are going to have to get more information to the Legislature.

COMPLAINTS
ABOUT TIME
PRESSURES

Many legislators admitted that more information alone would not get them out of their informational quandary. Although they generally wanted more detailed knowledge about the needs of colleges and universities, had more specific data been made available to them, they would not have been able to use it, simply because they did not have the time to read and absorb the materials. A member of the New York Ways and Means Committee suggested that additional legislative staff might alleviate some of the pressure, but went on to add:

> The question that then comes to mind is . . . if we had further staffing, to what extent could we fully utilize the products of the staffing. . . . I'm sure you appreciate the fact that higher education is only one of the many, many fields we are involved in. [We] worked all weekend on the budget . . . and we were working until 11:00 or 12:00 every night last week. . . . We've been on a treadmill for three or four weeks now, and there is a limit to physical capacity. . . . Assuming we had three or four men who could render their full attention to higher education, what would I do with their information? It would just be stacked up on the desk.

SUGGESTIONS
FOR BETTER
COORDINATION

Some respondents thought that the pressure of too little time for detailed study in all the areas where legislative decisions must be made could be partially alleviated by better coordination of the requests from the various state-supported institutions of higher education. Although many of the comments on this point were vague, most respondents seemed to think of coordination as some kind of prelegislative screening and distilling of information — either in special subcommittees or in special agencies outside the legislature. A member of the Iowa House Committee on Higher Education expressed this point of view. He felt that the existing system in which requests were channeled through the state board of regents was inadequate. Asked about ways to achieve better coordination, he replied: "The method hasn't been changed drastically or in basic form for almost a hundred years. . . . There must be some centralized organization." Another Iowan was critical of the fact that there was "very little coordination" of the needs of junior colleges with those of the major state colleges. He advocated "a more standardized form" of handling the requests of all state-aided colleges and universities to make the budgeting process "more understandable for the legislators."

A California leader expressed a similar desire for more coordination between the state's independent University and college systems. Asked about present practices, he felt that there was reasonable coordination within each system, but added: "It is only a haphazard sort of coordination. Between the colleges and universities there is practically none." Asked if there was need for more coordination, he replied: "From my own point of view I think there is. There should be some better statement of overall educational needs." Another Californian claimed that the Coordinating Council, established in 1961 to advise the Legislature and the executive on appropriations and planning, was not effective.

In Illinois, the Board of Higher Education, established by the Legislature in 1961, had evidently been more effective in screening and coordinating requests. Although most of the Illinois legislators with whom we talked indicated satisfaction with the way the board was functioning, a few complained, in the words of one, that "all this coordination" leaves them "woefully ignorant" on many aspects of higher education, and they lamented their loss of information and control.

ON BEING ON THE OUTSIDE

Dissatisfaction arising from the feeling of being outside the informed circle was a major theme that ran through the answers to our questions on the channeling and coordination of information and requests. Although some respondents complained that they did not have time to be as well informed as they would like to be, it appears that the more access they have to "firsthand" information—information direct from educational administrators and faculty—the more satisfied they are with the system. But when legislators feel that information—and effective decision-making power over educational appropriations—is beyond their grasp, they tend to be unhappy.

New York legislators seemed the most willing to let others handle the details of educational review and decision making. But even among New Yorkers some respondents wanted more detailed information on the nature of university needs and expenditures. The following dialogue with a member of the Senate Higher Education Committee is representative:

Interviewer: How are the requests of the separate institutions brought to the Legislature's attention?

Respondent: The State University comes in with a total budget request.

Interviewer: Are you satisfied with the way claims are presented to the Legislature?

Respondent: There's a very peculiar thing here. There isn't too much screening done by the Legislature, I must say, and I think it is one of the things we are at fault at. . . .

Interviewer: Would you say that you are satisfied with the prelegislative coordination that takes place?

Respondent: Not really. Why I'm saying "not really" is I don't think there is any member of this Legislature including the leadership and the chairman of the Finance Committee who really knows in depth what's happening at these . . . public universities.

Interviewer: Do you feel that the budget review is adequate?

Respondent: No. Absolutely not . . . I feel a little frustrated.

In Kansas the effective decisions on the allocation of state funds for higher education are apparently made by the Senate Ways and Means Committee. Legislators not on that committee believed they were not sufficiently informed nor permitted an important role in the appropriations process.

In Iowa formal requests from the state schools are relayed to the Legislature by the board of regents. Although Iowa solons reported that they relied on the regents for most of their information on the needs of the various campuses, they appeared a bit uneasy about doing so. A member of the Iowa House declared: "I sometimes wonder how good their judgment is. It is my impression that they've been somewhat overawed at times by the demands of the college presidents."

ON BEING ON THE INSIDE The comments of many legislative leaders suggested that they were happiest when they could find out about the needs of the colleges and universities on a relatively informal, firsthand basis. Many legislators attached great value to campus visits and personal conversations with school administrators and faculty. A Kansas state Senator said:

One school has made its needs known directly to me as chairman of a committee. And I have taken the committee down to view the problems firsthand. I think this is by all odds the best way to get information to us.

Yes, I would like to see more of this. . . . We are better able to deal with a problem if we have actually seen it, rather than see it in a fiscal report.

He went on to suggest that legislative tours—short campus tours with meals and entertainment—could be designed to provide legislative visitors with more useful firsthand information.

A member of the Texas House Appropriations Committee also emphasized the value of personal visits and contacts with university personnel. He reported that he received most of his information through personal conversations:

As a general rule, [I receive information] through talking with the individual presidents of the schools, sometimes the dean or a member of the board of regents or whatever kind of governing board they have. I have individual conversations with all of these people. And too, I have visited every campus in the state of Texas, and I have seen firsthand the condition of their physical situation. And I have rather close contact with all of the administrators.

Another Texas legislator reported the same kind of personal ties with educators. Clearly, these personal ties had a great deal to do with his "good feeling" about the information available to him. On the other hand, a third Texas legislator who had no personal contacts with educators, complained:

In my estimation, higher education people seem to pretty well talk to themselves. They don't talk to me. . . . This is really hard to take. Unless you go out of your way and really become interested, you really don't find out what the problems are. I think that the college professors as well as the college administrators ought to have us on their mailing list.

He wished educators would let him know not only what they were thinking about "the number one item of interest—money," but also "what they are teaching, what they are studying, and the things that bother them."

POLITICAL OBSTACLES Surprisingly few respondents complained that "politics" might prevent state legislators from being informed and from effectively reviewing the needs of colleges and universities. Only in Kentucky were our respondents almost unanimous in thinking politics interfered. A member of the Kentucky Senate Appropriations Committee summed up the feelings of others when he claimed that the Governor by-passed the legislature in the initial stages of budgetary review and allocation:

> By the time we received that information and began to study it . . . we found out that the Governor had already made certain reviews . . . and had allocated a specific amount of money to higher education and had returned the amount that he intended to include in the budget to the council for division among the colleges. So . . . our initial review was totally worthless.

A Pennsylvania House leader had a similar complaint. In Pennsylvania, he declared, the Legislature was never given an opportunity to examine the information the universities supplied.

Quite different considerations were voiced by some California legislators who hinted that "dirty politics" on the part of University officials hindered the process of effective budgetary review. A Republican Assemblyman declared:

> They used to get every cent they asked. But now they are meddling in politics and telling us a lot of lies. For example, when an official of high standing . . . sits where you are and privately admits that the University can live with a few million dollars less, and then he goes out and makes a public statement that they desperately need all that they requested—that's immoral! You can't have double standards in dealing with us, in requesting your budget, and still hold the confidence of the legislators. I find the University attitude on this incredibly naïve. Do they think they can still keep their political support here? They're all wrong if they do.

No hard and fast conclusions can be made as to just how much information a legislator should have to participate intelligently in the educational policy process. Probably, as in other areas of public policy making, it is the political salience of a particular area to a particular legislator that is most likely to determine the degree to which he will seek out information. And salience in politics, in turn, is largely a matter of considerations of party, constituency, and pressures from lobbyists. How much salience, then, does higher education have in the perceptual world of the state official?

CONSTITUEN-CIES AND CLIENTELES Most of our respondents indicated that the public did not demand much information from them on higher education. Indeed, communication between constituents and legislators in regard to higher education appeared to be almost nonexistent in many cases. Such exchanges as occurred tended to be sporadic and unorganized, usually dealing with some specific matter directly affecting a constituent's family or business, but not with higher education as an institutional concern of society.

One respondent said: "We hear from the voters only about the [secondary] schools; damn near don't hear from anybody about higher education. The only time I can think of we've heard anything much was when the new campuses were proposed."

The usual response to our question, "From whom in your constituency are you likely to hear about higher education?" was "the president of the university," or "members of the board of regents," or less frequently, "alumni and faculty members."

The average citizen did not feel a need to become involved in higher education, it appeared, unless an incident occurred directly relevant to him—the inability of his child to get into college, a highly publicized student demonstration, or perhaps a tax increase directly related to education.

An exception was campus unrest. Although our interviews were conducted prior to the disorders at Columbia University in spring, 1968, complaints about student demonstrations reported in the mass media were reaching legislators even then. It is likely, to judge from recent legislative action in many states to curtail the activities of student militants, that in this connection at least, legislators tend to fear the people's voice. (For a fuller treatment of legislative responses to campus unrest, see Chapter 8.)

On the whole, however, higher education has low political salience for state legislators because articulated demands from a broad section of the population are missing. As a result, policies and appropriations are less likely to be sacrificed in the kind of bargaining that occurs in policy areas where the stakes are seen as politically significant for survival. Therefore, the legislator as an individual and the legislature as a whole can more readily play the role of "trustee" in matters of higher education than might otherwise be possible. Lack of interest on the part of ordinary citizens, alumni, and special groups gives the legislature much freedom of action.

4. Control and Oversight in Higher Education

Along with lawmaking, appropriations, and representation, legislative oversight of administration is generally accepted as a legitimate function of the legislature in a system of separated powers. But just what oversight means, especially in particular instances; how it is to be distinguished from "control," "supervision," or "interference;" and how either oversight or control can or should be carried out are questions that puzzle the political scientist as much as the political practitioner. A simple definition, as the following attempt (Harris, 1964, p. 4) shows, does not help very much:

"Control" in the narrow sense refers to legislative decisions or activities prior to the relevant administrative action. Thus it includes legislative determinations about departmental policies and activities, examination of proposed executive actions in view of a possible legislative veto, and the issuance of authoritative instructions to guide executive officers in the performance of assigned functions. . . . "Oversight," strictly speaking, refers to review after the fact. It includes inquiries about policies that are or have been in effect, investigations of past administrative actions, and the calling of executive officers to account for their financial transactions.

In practice it is difficult to distinguish control from oversight, and for our purposes, a necessarily complex discussion of the problems involved is unneeded. For we have reasons to doubt that our legislative respondents were reacting in any strictly technical sense to the words "control" and "overseeing" that were used in our questioning. The responses given by the 88 state legislators in our survey generally confirmed an observation made some years ago in a study of 474 state legislators that neither "control" nor "oversight" are seen as principal legislative roles (Wahlke et al., 1962, p. 136):

In the four legislatures we are studying [California, New Jersey, Ohio, Tennessee], the major "object of the game" is recognized to be "legislation," the making of certain types of authoritative decision. Other purposes, functions, and objectives of legislative activity subsidiary, complementary, or independent of this there may be. But in these states the individual governing his actions wholly by these incidental objectives and not at all by the principal task of lawmaking is not considered to be acting as a legislator at all.

THE PROPER ROLE OF LEGISLATIVE CONTROL

How much control do state legislators feel they should have over higher education—in general and in regard to specific aspects such as admissions policies, curriculum, construction of new facilities, and so on? To elicit response, we first asked very general questions along this line: "How do you feel about the amount of control the Legislature has over higher education at the present time? Is it about right, too little, too much? Why?" If the respondent gave only general answers, we then asked him specific questions about legislative influence over admissions policies, curriculum, and construction.

From the answers, it appeared that there was considerable agreement on what constituted the proper legislative role in controlling higher education. Most legislators maintained that they should restrict their decision making to appropriations, and perhaps very general policy guidelines—such as stipulating that admissions policies should not discriminate among racial groups. The details of admissions policies, curriculum, and even construction of facilities were, they maintained, essentially "academic matters" best handled by officials better qualified, and less subject to parochial political pressures, than the legislators—the governor and his staff, the board of regents, independent coordinating boards, or administrators of individual colleges and universities.

Respondents generally classified decisions on anything but the most general aspects of admissions or curriculum policies, and even decisions to construct new buildings, as outside the normal sphere of legislative control. A Pennsylvania legislator put it succinctly: "The budget is the proper area for us to get involved in. We should stay out of curriculum and admissions." A second Pennsylvanian was equally concise: "We review the budget and check on the use of state funds. . . . We have not gotten into admissions standards and curriculum, and I don't think we should."

A California Assemblyman offered more extensive comments:

If you start controlling the curriculum, you control the end product. I'd sort of back away from that. I think that we have to; to a certain extent the Legislature should determine to what extent it wants to finance specialized kinds of education in the professional areas and law schools, medical schools, and that sort of thing. But it should be on a basis of evaluating recommendations made by the institutions themselves and by the Coordinating Council. I think the initiative ought to come there. And we have to evaluate these in terms of our set of priorities — what we can afford and what we can't afford.

An Iowa legislator agreed:

I'm satisfied with the [way] the board of regents are operating the schools . . . and I don't think the Legislature, aside from appropriating, and perhaps in a very general way recommending policies . . . should be poking our nose into the administration of the universities . . . the Legislature should not become too involved and too embroiled in the day-to-day operation of the university.

A New York committee chairman's position was almost identical:

I think it is the responsibility of the Legislature to look carefully into those [budget] requests. But once we have approved any particular plan . . . I think the Legislature should, well, not try to run things. . . . I think the administration of the educational process should not be controlled or dominated by the Legislature.

A Texas Representative expounded on the same theme:

I don't think that the Legislature should have any authority over the university other than that required to ensure that the money is spent honestly and that there is an accounting for all the public funds spent in the university. . . . We ought to decide how much money is necessary to run a university system . . . and then we ought to leave the rest of the system alone. . . . When we get into regulating what is going to be taught and how the students are going to be controlled, we are on very, very dangerous ground.

Legislators offered a variety of reasons for limiting their control to budgetary review. Many maintained that they must respect "academic freedom," or that "politics" should be kept out of higher education. Others emphasized that legislators were not qualified to make decisions on details of curriculum and administration and should leave such matters to "the professionals" — academic administrators and coordinating bodies.

The attitude that "the professionals" should handle decisions on admissions and curriculum policies was expressed by the Pennsylvania leader who told us: "I'm perfectly willing, as far as the academic curriculum and that sort of thing, to let the universities run themselves. . . . Some of the people are screaming about more controls. . . . I think we ought to stay away from that."

An Illinois leader seconded this view. He declared that although some legislators were "getting static from people who want to get in [to the university] and can't," the Legislature should not attempt to change admissions policies. He told us: "There's a growing feeling among the legislators that since we are providing the funds and all that we ought to have something to say [about admissions policies]. . . . I don't think that we should. I think that that should be left to the professionals."

An Iowa leader expressed confidence in the state's academic administrators:

I think the present [amount of legislative] control is sufficient. . . . Under the present setup . . . the Legislature . . . approves the amount of money spent, and I think that as of now, the Legislature has quite a bit of confidence in the administrators spending the money more wisely than the Legislature could spend it itself.

A Texas Senator agreed. If the Legislature did not like the way the "professionals" ran the system, he said, it should change administrations, not legislate educational policy. An Illinois leader was emphatic: "The only [legislative] control [over higher education] is in the field of money, and this is how it should be. You shouldn't have politics getting into higher education." A Kentucky legislator maintained that the statute which allowed the Legislature to determine the sites of new community colleges gave it too much control over what should be an "academic" decision: "I really think the site selection ought not to be a political matter. It ought to be a matter of need, based on study, and I don't think it ought to come before the Legislature."

Another Kentuckian expressed the common view that educators should be given as much autonomy as possible in matters of curriculum, and that legislators should respect the principle of academic freedom. A Kansas leader concurred:

I think there is a danger in having too much control. In some states that I read about and sometimes in our Legislature, some legislators tend to overemphasize the need for state control over higher education. I think we should provide the framework for them to work in, but we shouldn't overdo the control aspect and violate . . . academic freedom.

A Texas legislator was among those who emphasized that the Legislature was not qualified to make decisions on the details of admissions and curriculum policies. Even decisions on construction of new buildings were sometimes classified as the prerogative of educational professionals. A Pennsylvania Senator declared: "I don't think we should get into the business of admissions or curriculum, or even the construction of new buildings."

A Texas legislator agreed. The following exchange ensued:

Interviewer: What about admissions standards or curriculum? Do you think the Legislature has enough control?

Respondent: Yes, I do. I really do. I would like to leave as much of that type of authority to the individual institution and to the Coordinating Board as . . . possible. . . . Those people are giving their time [to higher education] every day of every year, and members of the Legislature are concerned with too many other things. . . . I certainly would want to leave that authority to them.

Interviewer: How about matters like construction of new buildings?

Respondent: Yes, the same thing.

Among the majority of legislators who maintained that legislative control of higher education should be primarily in the form of budgetary review and decisions on appropriations, many agreed with the Texas leader who told us, "This is all we really need," and with the Pennsylvania legislator who declared, "The Legislature has enough control . . . any time you can snap your fingers and hold onto the money you have considerable control." A New York legislator said:

I feel we control the purse strings. . . . If we ever wanted to stop the State University from doing something—I don't know what it would be—I feel we could do it that way. I have opposed almost every measure which would tighten up legislative control of the university.

An Iowa legislator maintained that line-item review of appropriations requests gave Iowa lawmakers all the formal control they needed over higher education. With respect to construction of new facilities he declared: "We [the Legislature] have an overriding [role] right now. As a matter of fact, we are the controlling factor in the construction of new buildings. . . . We say specifically, $3 million for such-and-such building."

Even in Illinois, where many legislators complained that they had become little more than a rubber stamp for the budgetary decisions of the governor and the Board of Higher Education, a lawmaker maintained that the Legislature's budgetary control was not only sufficient, but excessive.

LEGISLATIVE ABILITY TO OVERSEE Part of the legislators' expressed reluctance to be responsible for the details of academic policy making may well have stemmed from a realization that they were not in a position to do so. When we asked if the legislature was equipped adequately to *oversee* higher education, most respondents replied that it was not. They generally maintained that the executive was more capable than they and declared that the legislature lacked sufficient time, staff, and information even to conduct a detailed review of budgetary requests. The common view was summed up by one legislator who stated, "We haven't the time, the energy, nor the ability to supervise higher education," and by another who declared: "The executive . . . is more qualified for overseeing higher education. He has a competent staff. As far as the legislative branch itself, we are a part-time body. . . . I just don't think the legislative branch is equipped to do it."

Lack of information was frequently cited as a reason for legislative inability to review the budget adequately or supervise the details of college and university operations. An Iowa legislator commented that even members of key appropriations committees were ill-informed on budgetary matters:

I would say that the Legislature generally has little knowledge of what's going on. I was chairman of the regents' appropriations committee last time, and I doubt if anybody else in the Legislature was particularly aware of what the [university] askings were for. I wasn't even able to get my own committee to attend all the meetings.

The Legislators who were not on key committees were even shorter on information, observed several state leaders. A member of the Kansas House spoke for most of his colleagues when he told us: "We legislators . . . especially on the House side, do not get a full picture. By the time the information gets to us, it has been sifted so many times that we don't really know what the needs of the institutions are."

One of the many legislators who complained of being "swamped with work" explained that higher education was "only one of the many decision-making areas" with which legislators had to deal. A Kentucky legislator told us, "Very few of the legislators have any adequate knowledge of the budget," and concluded, "I think it's awful hard, if not completely impossible, to really have any indication of anything other than overall [budget] figures."

Almost none of the legislators interviewed admitted to being adequately staffed. A few, largely New Yorkers and Californians, felt they were better off than most state legislatures or that they were better staffed than in the past, but most maintained that effective oversight—even of the budget—was severely hampered by lack of legislative assistance. An Iowa committee chairman complained:

I don't think the Legislature is equipped to oversee hardly anything at the present time in Iowa. . . . The Legislature's understaffed and underpaid, and they don't have the people that give the legislators any unbiased recommendations.

A similar lament came from a New York Assemblyman: "We have a problem in this Legislature . . . with staffing our committees. There is a tremendous patronage pot, which this money we have for staff is used for, and as a result . . . all of our committees are understaffed." A colleague in the New York Senate agreed, adding: "We have to have some staff that can give us intelligent analyses. We can't expect to make judgments off the top of our heads on these matters without the proper people doing research."

A California legislator told us:

We are improving, California at least, our capacity to do things like this. I think we can dig in much deeper than we could before and perform the [oversight] function. But you haven't got that many elected representatives who have the ability to do it, and when you spread those with the best ability among all the other legislative responsibilities, you haven't got anybody left to do the job.

THE ROLE OF THE EXECUTIVE BRANCH Consistent with legislators' generally narrow definition of the role which they should, or could, perform in higher educational decision making were their comments on the role of the state executive and of special administrative bodies such as boards of regents or independent coordinating boards and councils. Most legislators seemed to want considerable guidance—either from the executive branch or independent administrative bodies or both—and to feel that they, rather than the legislature, should be the primary governmental force in higher education. A Texas leader expressed this theme when he told us:

[The Legislature] is not equipped by training or inclination; it doesn't have enough time [to deal with the details of higher education] . . . I think that we need to be given an outline of a program by the Coordinating Board. I think that we need to be helped to set the [general] goals of higher education.

A Louisiana legislator expressed views shared by several colleagues when he suggested that the executive strengthen its role as a liaison and intermediary between educators and Legislature: "No question about it . . . the executive branch, particularly in Louisiana, could help us have better communications and coordination with these universities and colleges."

An Iowa committee chairman expressed an attitude widespread among legislators—that the executive, not the Legislature, should set the pace for higher education in the state. The governor, he declared, "ought to have the main responsibility for higher education. . . . [He] ought to make recommendations to the Legislature. . . . If there is a weak governor, the Legislature will be weak also in matters of education."

A Kansas legislator took a similar position:

The executive branch [should have] the primary responsibility for reviewing the budgets and for establishing the general pattern of higher education and making its recommendations to the Legislature. For this fiscal year higher education has fared quite well in the executive. . . . In the past, [it has fared] both ways. Sometimes the executive recommendations have not been adequate from the college's point of view.

This last remark touches on another aspect of legislators' views that the governor should act as a supporter and protector of the college and university system. Legislators who appeared most willing to let the executive take a dominant role in overseeing higher education tended to be those who felt that the governor was a strong, effective, advocate of higher education. A New York Assemblyman was explicit on this point:

When you ask if I'm satisfied with the amount of control the Legislature has, I'm putting it in the frame of reference with a governor who is sensitive to the needs of higher education. If you had a governor who didn't have that sensitivity, who came in with budgets that were inadequate, and we raised them, and he vetoed them, under those circumstances then I would say we haven't enough control.

Several Texas leaders agreed with this position. Many praised Governor Connally's efforts to expand and improve the Texas system of colleges and universities, including a member of the Senate Finance Committee who told us:

The governor is the focus of public attention, and so, if he wishes and has the personality to do so, he can pretty well influence public opinion. I think that this has been Governor Connally's contribution to higher education. . . . He has made the public aware of the [needs], and I think that he presents this in such a way as to convince the public that the expenditures which have been made and which will be needed are proper and necessary —and that we are getting our money's worth. . . . Let me add that if it weren't for Governor Connally, I think that appropriations [for higher education] would be at least 20 percent less than they are now.

An Illinois legislator had similar praise for Governor Kerner:

In the past seven years in Illinois, the executive has taken the initiative and has brought forth a big part of the good things we have in higher education in Illinois. Governor Kerner has been outstanding in this area. It was at his insistence that the Board of Higher Education was initiated; it was at his insistence that the Illinois Building Authority was created, and without these two things, we would be topsy-turvy in Illinois today—and whoever the next executive is, I hope he is as strong as Governor Kerner has been. The Legislature, if they'd been left on their own, would have made a mess of the thing. But this is true of all legislatures.

Although most legislators felt that the executive did, or should, set the pace for state government supervision of higher education, their remarks indicated that they were far from willing to abdicate all control. As one legislator told us, the role of the executive "should be a matter of cooperative direction and providing facilities in consultation with the [Legislature] and the educators, but not dictating the programs." Though legislators tended to deny the existence of executive-legislative conflict over higher educational policies, their comments revealed that disagreement was, as one might expect, relatively common and that when legislators disagreed with executive policies or budget priorities, a test of relative political strength often ensued. An example of this was described by a New York Democrat who assured us that there was "no conflict" between the Legislature and the executive on educational policy. In the next sentence he reported:

The only field where there was real conflict had to do with the City University. Now two years ago, when we passed the City U Construction Act, the Governor fought this like hell, because he was determined that the City U should charge tuition, and this is one area where there has been tremendous conflict between the Legislature and the Governor. . . . We got into a tremendous conflict about that. . . . As a result of a series of circumstances, we were able to force the Governor . . . and the Republican majority in the Senate to go along with us. But beyond that there has not been any great conflict. The other area is the SEEK program where every year now we seem to have to fight with the Governor about the amount of money that should go into that.

A California Assemblyman indicated that the Legislature and the executive frequently did not see eye-to-eye on University appropriations. Given the Governor's item veto, he maintained, the executive's preferences generally prevailed:

The fact of the matter is right now the Legislature has almost no role to play in the University budget. The University negotiates with the executive. They proceed to recruit on the basis of what the executive tells them they can get and nothing else. Now I think that's a mistake. First of all I think the University ought to be devoting its energies to a two- or three-year advance budgeting, rather than this catch-as-catch-can on the current year. But a governor who wants to be tough about it and who has any pull at all in his own party, you know, when he comes out with a budget figure, that's it. You know we can propose something else, we did last year. And voted it into the budget. Then he comes along with his item-veto privileges and cuts it back down. And there's absolutely nothing we can do about it.

An Iowa Assemblyman was one of the few state leaders to report a specific example of conflict over a nonbudgetary matter. Asked whether the Legislature had sufficient control over the board of regents, he replied:

Well, yes . . . the Governor of course appoints them . . . but . . . the last session we turned down an appointment of the Governor's I led the opposition to the appointment. I don't think it was a sound appointment, or for the good of the state or the institutions. It was a political payoff, in my opinion, by the Governor. . . . I think the Senate acted wisely in this case, by rejecting the appointment.

LEGISLATIVE INTERFERENCE IN ACADEMIC AFFAIRS

The preceding comments on legislative-executive conflicts indicate that state legislators do not always follow the principle of noninterference in "academic matters" which they profess.

Reports of legislative efforts to control some aspect of higher educational policy with which they were unhappy were quite numerous. Similarly, there were predictions of legislative retaliation against administrators who failed to control student demonstrations and radical activities on campus. Legislators who told us about incidents of interference generally explained that the legislature had been "forced" to act, because the "professionals"—university administrators, or sometimes the state's coordinating board—had in some way neglected their responsibility for running the educational system in accord with the interests of the taxpayers.

A California Democrat expressed the attitude implicit in many of these comments. Asked if he would favor an increase in the amount of control that the Legislature had over higher education he replied:

I generally subscribe to the view of autonomy as far as the academic community is concerned, and I feel that we must rely on the people in education to make the decisions which affect education. That's about the best answer that I can give you, and I've tended to oppose efforts to use the purse strings to force the academic community into courses of action which it was reluctant to take. I do think though autonomy means responsibility, and I think that if higher education doesn't function responsibly and doesn't deal with these problems in a way which satisfies the public, which convinces the public that it's getting its so-called taxpayer dollar's worth, then there will be pressure on the Legislature to involve itself in higher education.

Kentucky legislators reported they had recently passed a bill raising tuition for out-of-state students and limiting out-of-state enrollment; but most agreed with the legislator who declared:

I don't think it's a legislative function, properly, until such time as the Legislature determines that things are out of hand. I think that occurred this last session. There was a great feeling among legislators that the out-of-state student situation had been permitted to get completely out of hand. . . . I think people in the Legislature were concerned about the fact that a great deal of the public taxpayers' money was being spent to educate children from out of the state of Kentucky, and not children within the state of Kentucky. . . . Preferably I'd like to see the Council on Public Higher Education function in that field.

Asked if, in general, the Legislature should take charge of other than budgetary matters, he continued:

I know of no other areas at the present time that the Legislature ought to control. I don't want to say that the Legislature should never step in and take charge of some function. For example, if the Council on Higher Education permits a helter-skelter graduate program to evolve in the various universities without a central coordinating factor, I think the Legislature is the last resort with regard to stepping in and doing something about it.

An Illinois respondent emphatically rejected the notion of legislative control over admissions and curriculum. His subsequent statements, however, were filled with examples of how legislators are sometimes "forced" to take action in these areas:

Just the other day I saw in the paper that the university board of trustees were trying to help out the underprivileged again. Somebody had introduced a resolution and they passed it to lower the standards for some of the underprivileged. Now I got right on the phone and got ahold of the president—I've known him for years, he's a good friend—I got his secretary and I told her I was coming to see him that day. It was Saturday. And I went over and saw him. I told him that he couldn't do that. Suppose some farmer's boy with better qualifications doesn't get in and those who aren't qualified do get in? How do you explain that to the public? . . .

Another case. Twenty-five years ago we passed a statute in the Legislature—I had a hand in it. It prevented subversive groups from advertising in university facilities or using university buildings and the like. This statute was on the books for 19 years, and the university administration enforced it, and there wasn't any trouble. Those SDS came along and brought pressure on the trustees, and the trustees recommended repealing the law. Now the state Senate adopted a resolution about that, and the board backed down. Is the University of Illinois going to be a place where every guest of the university that some slob doesn't like, or just a few slobs don't like, is going to get hooted down when he tries to speak? When he's been invited? At the embarrassment of 90 percent of the students and the university? Now you see from these cases that the Legislature only goes in when things get too far out of line. A tax-supported institution has got to be run the way the public wants. But these things never should have happened. It's not the Legislature's job.

A Texas leader who thought that the Legislature's control over the colleges and universities was "about right" described how members of the Legislature had attempted to get a controversial professor dismissed:*

I think that it is shameful, as happened last week, that a member of the House should write a telegram and send it to the board of regents asking the dismissal of a professor. That is the board of regents' business. Or, more correctly, it is the [university] administration's business. . . .

He went on to relate how several legislators "wanted a bill passed last [session] to keep guns out of the students' residences . . . the [university] administration should take care of this. They can tell them where they can keep them. . . . The Legislature should not get into that."

The most frequently cited instances which led legislators to seek detailed control over academic affairs, or at least over specific situations, were student demonstrations and what legislators termed "radical activities" on state campuses. An Iowa legislator's comments were fairly representative of those who warned of legislative retaliation against irresponsible faculty and administrators:

I'm not one who believes in interfering with the administration of the institutions, and I've fought some attempts to interfere. But the Legislature has tremendous control over the money. And I'm sure that some of the things that have been happening on our campuses in the last year are going to have a real effect on the Legislature when they control the purse strings next time. I would think the people of Iowa and the nation are fed up with some of the wild-eyed professors and the draft card burners and so forth, and some of this activity that's done in the name of academic freedom. . . . But I'm sure that many legislators and many people around the Legislature this [session] are going to make this sort of thing an issue, and it's bound to affect appropriations. Whether it's good or bad, it's a political reality.

*The Legislature was successful. The professor was fired.

California legislators were especially vocal on the subject of radical activities on campus. Irritated by what they perceived as University contempt for legislative politics and pressured by constituents unhappy with student demonstrations and campus disruption, several California respondents indicated that they, or their colleagues, had about reached the limits of self-restraint. As one legislator declared:

At times like the present, it is only with the utmost restraint that I refrain from saying I would like to have more control. But I happen to have been around long enough and have great respect for the institution known as the University of California, which became great before the beatniks and the great liberals and the Savios and the demonstrations. And I hope it will remain great in spite of them. . . . But as I've told them, the same way on this campus police issue and everything else, I say "For God's sake please assume the responsibility which is yours" [before the pressures] from outside, from the people of California who still own the University, the people . . . in whom repose the residual interest which is being held in sacred trust by the regents . . . and the pressures from within myself [get so strong that I] just can't stomach it any longer.

Legislative frustrations were discussed at length by a California committee chairman, who said such frustration was widespread among his fellow legislators. He denied legislators wanted more control over things like curriculum—"I don't think they want that"— and he said, "I don't think they should either." He went on to say:

I guess every legislator has been hammered and hammered on the youth upsets and disturbances on campuses. . . . The constituents [demand that the Legislature] do something about it and do something about it now. . . . The legislator who can't do too much to control . . . the University system is apt to slash out trying to hit their budget. . . . It's not any logical way to do this but . . . it's the way some of these people feel . . . they'll strike back at finance. This is the only area where they can strike back. I think they will tend to cut and chop [if they] get into the spot where they can do it.

Yes. We've just gone through that with an investigation on the Fullerton State College campus . . . drama department. Now I don't know whether it is proper to do this or not—I'm not convinced it is. The frustrations of the committee who made the study—who went to the campus! They were harassed—the audience harassed them, the personnel before the committee harassed them. The committee were told they had dirty minds—this type of thing. And these men came back absolutely furious about the way they were treated. And the only way they could see to get to this is to chop with the fiscal ax. I don't think this is necessarily the way to attack the problem. There must be better ways than this. You don't cripple an institution. . . . [By] making it weak or destroying it . . . you don't solve the problem. But the . . . state taxpayers' monies are being used for things that state taxpayers cannot condone. . . . The legislators . . . are going to respond to this.

CONCLUSION   Most legislators felt that most aspects of higher education were the proper domain of the relevant executive agencies or the universities themselves and that it would be improper for them to get entangled in educational decision making. Where, in their view, the legislature was properly involved—the matter of funding—they felt that the built-in controls of the appropriations process were sufficient.

On the other hand, with regard to oversight, the constraints on legislative activity were seen to stem mainly from lack of staff and lack of time. In general, our respondents preferred not to "interfere" in the business of the state colleges and universities, and those who did evidently feel that they were "forced" to do so by irresponsible faculty, students, or administrators.

The overall impression was that state legislators were satisfied with existing relationships between the legislature and other state agencies in regard to higher education, and they appeared to have a sound sense of reality with respect to their own ability or inability to influence the course of educational decision making.

5. Financing Higher Education

Although it is not formally recognized as such, the educational enterprise—from elementary to higher education—is part of the nation's political economy. Like other sectors of the economy it must be capitalized and subsidized, and it is expected to be productive.

But, unlike other sectors, the educational enterprise does not readily lend itself to cost accounting. While the nation's expenditures on education can be precisely measured in dollars and cents, the outputs of the economy's educational sector defy easy measurement. Insofar as American society is willing to finance education, it is not only because education is assumed to contribute to the nation's economic wealth, but also because it is assumed that other values are obtained by an effective educational system. At stake are the benefits each citizen may derive from being as well educated as his abilities permit, as well as the moral, political, and survival capabilities of the nation. In some respects, therefore, support of an extensive and more than simply adequate educational system is an act of faith—the faith that education is perhaps the most critical item on the agenda of national needs.

Higher education alone requires expenditures of a size that can perhaps be appreciated best if one compares total expenditures for higher education from all public and private sources with the gross national product. In 1966, for instance, these expenditures amounted to $15.2 billion, or about 2 percent of the gross national product. High as this figure may appear to be in absolute dollar terms, it is clearly a relatively small item from the perspective of the economy as a whole. And it takes no cognizance of the much greater indirect contributions that higher education makes to the economic well-being of the nation through its training functions, its scientific research, and its technological innovations.

It is readily apparent from projections of enrollment and manpower needs that, in the future, expenditures for higher education from all sources must be substantially increased. An expanding population is likely to demand more college education, and a technologically advancing economy has increasing needs for skilled manpower. The Office of Education estimates that total enrollments in institutions of higher learning will increase from 5.5 million in 1965 to 9.0 million in 1975, of which 88 percent are expected to be undergraduates and 12 percent graduate students (U.S. Department of Health, Education, and Welfare, 1967). Graduate education, in turn, must provide the talent needed to teach in the colleges and universities. Requirements for scientists and engineers are expected to rise from the 1.3 million scientists and engineers employed in 1963 to 2.1 million needed in 1975 (U.S. Department of Labor, 1966).

The states' contribution to the financing of higher education is a cause for neither optimism nor pessimism. According to a report of the National Association of State Universities and Land-Grant Colleges for 1967-68, the states appropriated $4.4 billion in tax funds for the operating expenses of their institutions of higher learning compared with an appropriation of $1.4 billion in 1959-60 — an increase of over 200 percent. The report predicts that further increases are not likely to create hardship "because some of the gains come automatically from economic growth without changes in taxation. The state revenue systems are susceptible of almost constant improvement to make them more productive and more equitable, and can become thrice as productive as they now are"* (National Association of State Universities and Land-Grant Colleges, 1968).

Are state politicians equally sanguine? To find out, we asked our respondents a series of questions about the funding problems of higher education, beginning with an open question allowing them to express themselves freely, followed by specific questions requiring a good deal of relevant knowledge. We shall introduce the questions in context.

MONEY: A MAJOR PROBLEM Allowing respondents to express their concerns freely has the virtue of revealing their saliency. To maximize spontaneity, we initiated the interview with an open-ended question: "How do you feel things in higher education have been going in (state) over the past few

---

*These figures include appropriations to hospitals, experimental stations, and other facilities run by universities that are not directly educational in objectives.

years? What are some of the major problems?" Only if respondents were at a loss in answering were they asked "probing" questions, such as, "How about enrollment increases? How about financing? How pressing do you feel these problems are?"

Only a handful of legislators did not see financing as the major problem. An Education Committee chairman in Texas spoke for the minority:

Of course . . . we really don't have any financing problems as far as higher education or public schools are concerned. . . . We rank forty-second in the entire nation in per capita taxes and . . . we still don't have a state income tax or a sales tax in most of our cities yet. We don't have a corporate tax. We have plenty of areas in which we can expand taxes yet.

A legislator from Kansas declared, "Based on past experience in the state, the financing of higher education has never been a serious problem." A staff member of the Joint Legislative Committee on Higher Education in California felt that the most serious problem was the access of the students to the facilities rather than financing, although he conceded that "financing of new programs is a serious problem, there's no question of that." A Senator from New York agreed: "In the public sector, financing is not the biggest problem. I think we are supporting our public universities very well."

But most respondents saw "money" as the primary problem for higher education in their states. Some, without much elaboration, simply stated that getting higher education financed was the main difficulty. A member of the Kentucky Senate Appropriations and Revenue Committee, in a reply typical of many, remarked:

I would expect this [problem] would be one that faces all facets of government — money. I think that would be one of the major problems. I'm certain there are others, but this would be the big one in my opinion.

Quite a few respondents, however, without being prodded, gave specific reasons or mentioned specific circumstances which they felt to be at the root of the money problem. Another Kentucky Senator, for instance, brought up the matter of meeting enrollment increases:

If we must continue to raise the funds here in Kentucky to support this increase [in enrollment] at the level that it's presently being supported, I for one hardly see where the money is going to come from.

A Texas Senator, a member of the Finance Committee, said:

Well, of course, the biggest problem would be getting the methods and means to continue to finance higher education which is going to be necessary due to the growth of the population. The explosive growth of the population is such that, as I understand it, Texas now ranks third in population of people up to age 21. So we are going to need additional facilities to take care of the population explosion.

An Illinois legislator closely connected with policy making in higher education linked the need for more financing with the problem of recruiting competent teachers at the elementary and secondary school levels:

Yes, I think the problem is going to continue to be two things: money and competent teachers or instructors, and they both go back to money. If we could pay our teachers more after they become teachers to teach in the high schools and grade schools, we'd have more young people entering the teaching professions, and then we would have more in higher education because they could earn more. . . . You know, Illinois this biennium appropriated over a billion dollars for higher education. Now, if it weren't for the fact that we had the Illinois Building Authority who have authority to sell bonds to build buildings, our appropriations would have been much higher, or we would have done without a lot more.

Competition among the universities within the state and the influx of out-of-state students were seen as part of the money problem by a Kentucky Senator, a member of the Revenue and Appropriations Committees:

One of the things that I've been concerned about is the increasing cost of higher education. We apparently seem to be engaged in a race between some of our universities to see who can have the grandest institution, and of course, this costs money. And the question is where does the money come from. Now to pinpoint some of the concerns that I have, I think I can say one point would be in the area of graduate study. Another point would be in the area of nonresident students. . . . As a laymen who is not an educator it would seem to me that it would be more economical to assign graduate areas to some of the schools. . . . In the other area that I mentioned, that of nonresident students, it seems that we have pretty well put our barriers down, and we've allowed anybody to come to the state of Kentucky to go to our schools. This would be very fine if we were a wealthy state. Unfortunately, we are not a wealthy state, and it's costing us quite large sums of money to be able to educate these nonresident students.

In California, the administration of Republican Governor Ronald Reagan came in for criticism from Democrats who felt that funds were deliberately held back from educational institutions. One respondent remarked:

The area of finance particularly [is a problem]. It's the most important area. You can't run anything without money and the administration last year item vetoed the budget for the University to less than what the Governor had originally requested himself—and the state colleges too. Not nearly enough money was given. We're falling further and further behind in our competitive situation regarding faculty salaries with other states, and I believe we're now down around 13 in the University and down around 39 with the state colleges.

Asked whether this was due to the attitudes of the present administration, he replied: "Almost entirely . . . I think the previous administration was really committed to first-rate public higher education in California. I don't think this one is at all."

A Democratic leader of the Assembly in California said he did not see funding as a major problem right now except:

insofar as it involves overcoming the Governor's reluctance to fund higher education. . . . I can't quite read the Governor's motivation in all this. If I believe that they were consciously planning a program, I would have to believe that they picked on those areas of public interest which would be most vocal in their protestations against budget cuts in the belief that if they stepped on the toes of those people who were best able to scream that they could, therefore, best establish themselves as economizers. That seems to me to be what they've done in the field of higher education and mental health.

Finally, there were respondents who blamed the universities' financial difficulties on past failures of state government. For instance, a member of the Appropriations Subcommittee on Higher Education in Iowa said:

Had we been doing each biennium what we needed to do, this wouldn't be nearly as noticeable; we wouldn't have to have had a hundred million like we had the last session for state schools, and I think this kind of reverses, goes right back to our higher education because I've looked over our expenditures and . . . of course I get right back to what I was talking about a minute ago, and that was financing. This is actually the crux of the whole thing . . . keeping adequate finance to do what needs to be done, and as I said . . . one of our things is . . . finance for our board of regents.

Quite a few respondents in all states used the opportunity to discuss their state's tax problems. A California Assemblyman took a particularly gloomy view:

[Financing] is going to be a tremendous problem even more so than it is at the moment where we have got some critical problems because the state simply does not have enough resources in their revenue structure to pay for all services of state government that the people apparently want. One of the high priorities would be higher education, but there isn't going to be the same amount of money proportionately available to higher education as there once was.

One of the common themes among Illinois respondents was the necessity for tax reform, possibly a state income tax, to help with financial problems. A member of the Senate Education Committee and Budgetary Commission suggested that "until we get an income tax in this state, we're going to be in serious trouble on finance." An executive official said:

Well, the major problem is coming up. I would think we are going to be in the area of financing because the state has not overhauled its tax structure for a good many years. We're not going to be in the middle of a financial crisis, perhaps, but certainly a severe reassessment of expenditures. . . . I don't necessarily see any cutbacks or withdrawals from the support of higher education because of this, but I think that there are going to be problems.

Another high administrative official saw only one way to solve the state's financial squeeze:

by raising taxes. Through the Illinois Building Authority we've been reasonably successful in selling bonds. I don't know what the immediate future holds, however. A recent decision of the Supreme Court [declaring a new tax unconstitutional] poses some severe problems for the financing of Illinois governmental programs. . . . In the last session, our universities began to sense a feeling that the junior colleges are getting too much of the dollar.

A Kansas Senator thought that revenue for higher education must continue to come from nonproperty tax sources, such as sales and income taxes: "Only construction comes from the property tax, and I am saying even more so in the future education will depend on revenue from the general revenue fund of the state. The general revenue fund is based on the sales and incomes taxes." A New York Assemblyman criticized his state's "pay-as-you-go" program and advocated bonding with state guarantee of the debt:

> Well, of course, the major problem has been money. In this state we seem to be in a financial bind. Over the past few years, our future financial planning has not been dealt with as it should be. It seemed for awhile under the present administration — we've had a so-called pay-as-you-go program which turned out to be a real flop . . . very little was being done because he had that attitude. Good financial planning doesn't require that; I think we could have done a good deal with bonding and incurred the debt through the state rather than what he did after the pay-as-you-go program. After that, he decided to start with those gimmicks such as the creation of the authorities, and gave the authorities the right to issue their own bonds . . . without the full faith and credit of the state behind them. As a result, we have incurred a larger amount of interest charges over and above what would have normally been the case.

Finally, the chairman of a Senate Appropriation Committee in an Eastern state suggested that those benefiting from higher education, i.e., those in the higher income brackets, should pay for it:

> I think we haven't hit the right source of paying for higher education. . . . We can't continue to tax everybody for the education of those who are qualified and who will have the big income. We can't tax people for that purpose. We'll have to come down to the place where we will require the general tax funds that are put up for the education of certain individuals . . . that they repay it when they get into this higher income bracket.

As this review suggests, most state politicians perceived funding as the critical issue in higher education. This was not surprising because appropriations are the major concern of state legislators in the educational field.

COMPETITION FOR THE TAX DOLLAR One way of stimulating relevant responses is to provide the interviewee with a comparative frame of reference. We therefore asked this series of questions:

> How is the funding of higher education affected by the needs of other programs in the state? Just how is it affected? Where do you think is more need for funding here in (state) — in the primary and elementary schools or in higher education? Is there much competition between the institutions of higher learning and the lower-level school systems?

Many of the respondents hedged on some questions, saying that "each program gets what it seems to need," or "elementary and secondary education is really more important anyway," or "higher education does better than many other programs." But many frankly acknowledged the competition among state-financed programs and often cited "tight money" as the principal cause.

Competition among Levels of Education In general, respondents in several states confirmed the existence of competition between various levels of education, but they saw different reasons and held different attitudes. Respondents in Kentucky most often mentioned competition for state funds between higher and lower education. One legislator told us, "There is definitely competition of this kind. . . . The amount of money available for education is limited." Another Kentuckian declared:

You, right now, have a real fight in Kentucky between primary-secondary education and higher education. I've heard any number of public school teachers complaining about higher education getting the lion's share of the tax money. Of course they don't realize that this is the only place the colleges can get their money; they can't go to the localities for aid, because it is a state college or a university, a state function. . . . But the university does need to do a better job of public relations; in fact, all the state universities need to. The regional universities do a better public relations job, on an individual basis, than the University of Kentucky does, because they have presidents who, though they are educators, have a political background in Kentucky.

An influential member of the House Education Committee in Kansas said:

Certainly [there is competition with secondary schools]. As we say down on the farm, "When two or three pigs get in the same trough, they're all competing with one another." Well, that's the fact of life. . . . I'm sure that the regents, the chancellor, and all are not competing in the sense that they would want us to do less for public schools so that they could have more resources [themselves].

Not only were New York respondents sensitive to competition between higher and lower levels of public instruction, but they were also much concerned with possible competition between the expanding State University system and the state's private institutions.

Some legislators said that elementary and secondary schools deserved more support than higher education. An Illinois Representive, who thought that competition did not exist between the two, felt that public schools needed more at the time. A knowledgeable colleague acknowledged the existence of competition, but said: "Of course, you balance out as best you can the dollar. You give to each what you think in your judgment at this time they deserve."

A Representative from Kentucky thought that most legislators considered the lower levels of education more important than higher education. A colleague said:

I don't think higher education is affected at all now. It is doing pretty well, relatively speaking. I don't think it has been competing with primary and secondary education now, and there may be some conflict in the future, but it has not occurred yet. Whether they conflict or not depends on the willingness of the Legislature to let the local government units use something other than the ad valorem tax for schools.

Competition with Other Programs In addition to being asked about competition for the tax dollar between higher and lower education, state officials were asked about competition between higher education and other state programs. Some acknowledged that such competition existed, most claimed that it did not, and a few predicted that it soon would.

A member of Iowa's House Education Committee said:

Oh, definitely, definitely there's competition. . . . The outside competition from such things as conservation and the highway commission and so forth, all have a part in this, because where you're looking for $5 million for a pet project, perhaps we're talking of an increase in appropriations for higher education, 20 million; well, if we can shave that to 15, there's the 5 million this group's looking for. And so this competition always develops. And it's probably a healthy competition, because it forces justification, and this is always essential.

An Iowa Senator thought the board of regents had done well in convincing the Legislature of the priorities of higher education.

A California Senator said:

Well, a specific example, I coauthored a bill to get more funds for the water projects. I found this would mean a decrease in funds for higher education, and I asked to get off the bill.

He went on to say that there was no competition between higher education and lower levels because "I think they run into a conflict in terms of the legislative enactment." Several California respondents mentioned competition with medical services and welfare in the state. A legislative staff member said: "Because higher education has been for many years, and will continue to be, a tremendous growth area, it will compete with other major growth areas such as health, medical service, and welfare." A third Californian felt that the competition was due to the attitudes of the University people themselves:

Yes, there's now a great deal of competition. And this is new. Because of academic arrogance. You know we're all human beings. But I can show you statements where some of the University people have told us, in response to our request for information about budget requests and other things, "It's none of your damn business. All you do is simply to give us the funds and we will do the rest." This is terrible; who the hell do they think they are? They want all of the benefits, without taking any of the responsibility. . . .

I tell you, last year when the state college professors came to Sacramento to demonstrate in front of the Governor on the steps of the capitol, with their academic robes and with beards, people here were fed up. Certainly there is competition, and it's because the universities have created it. We in the Legislature are certainly taking closer looks at the budgets this year, and I think there is a good chance of reducing the higher education budget even below what the Governor is requesting.

A Texas Senator pointed out that competition among programs existed because funds for education were not dedicated, and thus educators had to justify any increases:

Well, of course, the higher education people come before the various committees in the Senate and the House and they try to justify whatever increases to them. I was talking about a dedicated tax for highways and roads out of gasoline taxes. And when I say they are earmarked, I mean that there is no way that a legislator can get in there and put one penny of that money into education.

Another Texan, a member of the lower house, thought the money was always spent on higher education and did not seem to approve of the constraints placed on other expenditures:

Well, of course, [higher education] is affected some [by the needs of other programs]. How much, I don't know. . . . I would say in general that absolutely essential expenditures of the universities are made regardless of what else goes on. I think that there are two kinds of things which have had money spent on them regardless of whatever else had to be done. That is the public universities, colleges, and various kinds of old-age assistance. Now the old-age-assistance program is still scandalous, but the old folks are a powerful voting bloc. . . . I would say that the universities have been held back by some other programs, but not much. Over 52 percent of the budget is spent on education.

Competition arising from demands on the general revenue fund was discussed by a House member in Illinois:

Well, basically all the money for higher education that the Legislature appropriates comes from the so-called general revenue fund. This is the state's basic source of revenue. Of course, the universities have tuition and federal grants and other income sources besides just the general revenue appropriations we make. . . . Of course, also making a demand on the general revenue fund are the common schools. Grammar schools and high schools, the mental hospitals, the basic operations of state government other than road building, all have to come out of general revenue. . . . Of course there's competition there.

Many legislators thought that higher education came out pretty well in competition with other programs. A member of the House Committee on Higher Education in Illinois said that when there was a bind, budgets were cut down generally. Others were even more optimistic about how well higher education fared in their states. A Senator, also from Illinois, thought there was a lot of competition, but that higher education was not affected:

There's a lot of it! Now, take this question of mental health. And it isn't so much higher education; there's always more demand for elementary education down here at the Legislature. . . . No sir, I don't think there's too much effect on higher education, not the competition.

The variety of perceptions, differing within as well as between states, was considerable. On the whole, however, legislators and other state officials thought higher education held its own in the competition for funds, either when competing with lower-level education systems or with other state programs. In general, our respondents certainly did not feel that higher education was disadvantaged vis-à-vis other state commitments, and they seemed to feel that higher education was at least as important as other programs.

ADDITIONAL FUNDING NEEDS: PRIORITIES To discover in more detail state officials' sensitivity to the needs of higher education, we asked a direct question about where, in their opinion, "the greatest need for additional funding" lay. Not surprisingly, most respondents saw a need in most areas—facilities, salaries, and scholarships—and also in regard to vocational schools, technical schools, junior colleges, or a combination of these. Very few legislators felt that present allocations were sufficient.

Construction The need to allocate new funds for construction was most frequently mentioned, and it was usually coupled, as in the following comments by two New York Assemblymen, with enrollment pressure: "Construction is very much needed, because you find that there is not enough room for those who want to go. I think that is the main one, and of course, from that follow the others;" and "I think we need the facilities to handle more students." Another New Yorker felt that existing institutions should be enlarged and new institutions created. A member of the Pennsylvania House Committee on Education felt that facilities were urgently needed to take care of the students already coming to the universities:

If we can get more funds, I think we need to use these funds to expand the facilities that we have now. [At] Penn State U and the state colleges and Indiana U, our problem is not to attract more students. Our problem is to get more facilities so that we can take care of the students who have already applied.

Similar observations were made by many respondents in all states and to cite more would be repetitive.

Faculty Salaries Perhaps next in importance was a recognition that additional funds were needed for faculty salaries. No respondent felt that present salary levels were sufficient. An Illinois Representative thought: "We've got a pretty good balance now. Faculty salaries are getting up into the ball park where they ought to be. They're maybe not quite there yet, but they're getting there." But some respondents felt that the issue was more urgent. A Kansas legislator said:

I think [additional funding] ought to be in the salaries. . . . Maybe I'm biased. I sometimes think the state of Kansas spends thousands of dollars promoting Kansas as an industrial site to attract industry. I think it wou.d be fascinating if we would take another approach and pay a very nice salary to college people and staff KU with some of the best brainpower in the country.

Another Kansan reported hearing from the heads of the universities that, given present salary levels, "it is very hard to maintain the kinds of staff that are required to make the university great." A Texas respondent who felt that the state's building program was a sound financial basis thought that "the only question remaining then is money for salaries, which has got to come out of our general revenue fund."

A Pennsylvania legislator astutely saw a close link between the need for better salaries to attract teachers and the need for student subsidies:

I don't see the need for better funding in construction simply because this has been proceeding well. . . . I think there is a definite need for additional funds for teacher salaries, of course, faculty compensation, and just to handle the growth of the student body, which is going to take more supplies, more teachers, more administrative expense, more general operating expense, and more scholarships. Right now we're up to about 40 million annually in our scholarship program, and there are an awful lot of children in this commonwealth who have the intellectual capacity to pursue a higher education but don't have the financial ability to do so who are deprived of pursuing a higher education because they don't have the funds. I think it's to these children that we have to address ourselves in terms of more funds from the commonwealth.

Scholarships and Loan Programs Relatively few respondents gave priority to additional funding of scholarships or loan programs, perhaps either because they thought present state programs were adequate or because they expected the federal government to take care of student subsidies. A New York Assemblyman gave high priority to scholarships for the poor:

I think scholarship aid for the very poor, and additional considerations for the poor, is primary. Faculty salaries I'm not so sure about. I think the

State University is being realistic about this and is keeping up. Construction—I think when we build, we should build good buildings, because heaven knows when we'll be able to build again. The fact that we spend a lot of money on buildings doesn't particularly bother me.

Several other New York Assemblymen thought that scholarships should be increased because salaries and construction were already well endowed. A Senator from Iowa thought that long-term investment loans should be available for all students as the best method of financing education.

Research A few respondents placed further funding of research high on the list of priorities, usually in connection with faculty salaries, apparently on the assumption that research funds are as significant to many university professors as their personal support. But, in general, research funding did not appear an imperative need in the perspective of state legislators. A California respondent thought that "right now we ought to [restore] the research function of the University to a higher level. And then the next debt is for faculty salaries." A Texas respondent felt that salaries, scholarships, and research were all important needs.

New Institutions Although we shall deal with the problems of creating new institutions in later chapters, it should be pointed out that in Texas and Iowa some respondents used this opportunity to express concern for the development of junior colleges and vocational and technical schools. An Iowa respondent suggested: "Well, certainly these new vocational-technical community colleges are going to require millions of dollars to really get adequately funded. And this is the big need."

Similarly, a Texas legislative leader emphasized the societal benefits of development schools of a practical nature: "It's like I have said before, it's right down with the junior colleges at the vocational level. That's where they have a direct line to the troubles on the street; they can deal with social problems there with job training."

On the whole, our attempt to elicit what funding priorities seemed important to legislators was disappointing. But this should not come as a surprise. Modern legislative bodies are rarely policy-initiating agencies; rather, they respond to the demands that are made on them, and it is perhaps inappropriate to expect legislators to anticipate possibilities that are not within practical feasibility. In general, politicians do not like to deal with hypothetical alternatives. By far the majority of our respondents saw funding needs in several areas and refused to place one above the other.

SUGGESTED SOLUTIONS TO MONEY PROBLEMS There was good reason to assume that politicians' views on raising new funds for higher education would be greatly influenced, among other things, by their state's existing tax structure and tax burdens. At the time of this survey, for instance, 7 states still had no general sales tax, 13 were without an individual income tax, and 11 had no corporate income tax. Moreover, in many states the effectiveness of taxes was limited by exemptions of one kind or another. In response to the question, "What means do you see are available to increase revenue for higher education?" state legislators gave a variety of answers. They also differed on increased student tuition as a way to solve the money problems.

Taxes and Bonds Our concern here is not with the distribution of responses, pro or con, for our survey does not permit of measurement. Rather, our purpose is to convey a sense of legislators' concern and involvement. Some, for instance, were simply resigned to accept new taxes as a fact of life. An Iowa respondent said, "The only way you can pay for this [higher education] in government is taxes . . . so you're going to have to raise taxes." Similarly, those opposed to new taxes were brief. Another Iowan, for instance, did not see any need for increased or new taxes because "as school expenses increase, so should revenue from present sources." Surprisingly, the fear of raising taxes or introducing new taxes in an election year was hardly mentioned at all.

In states such as Texas where tax options were still wide open, respondents sometimes even sounded enthusiastic over the prospect of tapping new sources. As one respondent put it: "I personally think that we have been very reticent about getting into what I think is the most excellent system of taxation, the state income tax. We haven't even touched it here in Texas." Another Texan rejected tuition increases and suggested both an individual and corporate income tax as making for a "more flexible system." A third Texas legislator favored a sales tax and the elimination of exemptions:

If you want my personal opinion, I think that we need a full expansion across the board with the sales tax, and I think that would come close to solving our problems for the next 10 years. And by across the board, I mean eliminating almost every exemption now in the sales tax and including food. Also, then you can increase the rate. Texas is at 2 percent, which is among the lowest in the nation.

Bonds, it seems, were so widely used as a source of revenue in the states surveyed that they were hardly mentioned as a feasible alternative. Only in Kentucky did we discover disagreement. One respondent emphasized that he was "not against using bonds at all," and thought "they should be used to their maximum." But another respondent said: "I think we have gone as far as we can with general bond issues. . . . We cannot do much along these lines." No respondent discussed the advantages or disadvantages of bonds as such.

Of course, some favored a combination of various methods of raising new funds. A Kansan said:

We have a lot of nuisance taxes and small taxes and sin taxes [whiskey and cigarette taxes] and all, but the real revenue to run the state and local government has got to come from income. And this means income and sales taxes. The sales tax is the poor man's income tax. The combination of the two is probably the fairest.

A Californian felt that the whole tax structure needed overhauling: "I think we are going to have some significant tax changes. We can't let these insurance companies and oil companies off as free as they got off last year with that tax bill. And we could bring in a substantial amount of money from withholding." But a colleague differed: "Well, I hope we continue to rely on the general tax structure."

Federal Aid to Higher Education

Legislators were similarly split on federal aid. Whether in favor of or opposed to federal aid, few saw it as a substitute for state support.

Almost no federal policy is as complicated as aid to education. Quite apart from many baffling technical problems, the question of participation of the national government in the educational enterprise has long been bewitched by constitutional controversies, such as the church-state issue or the civil rights issue, that were in many respects extraneous to the problems of education as such.

While the allocation of federal resources to education is now generally considered essential, if for no other reason than that the federal government has them and the states do not, and while many of the constitutional obstacles have been removed, the would-be danger of "federal control," as our survey revealed, continues to linger in the minds of many state officials. Whatever objections opponents of federal aid may have for substantive reasons, they apparently still find it congenial to express themselves in the language of "states' rights." To this is often added nowadays the fear of the federal bureaucracy tying up educational development in red tape and imposing constraints on a "free" system which, somehow, is thought to be safeguarded by the states.

Our purpose in asking the questions we did ask was not to elicit factual information about the working of federal aid in the various states, but to discover legislators' or executive officials' feelings, appraisals, suggestions, perceptions, and expectations with regard to the subject. We therefore asked the following questions:

- Federal aid now comes in many forms. In general, how do you feel about federal aid to higher education?

  Probe: Do you have any view as to what kinds of federal aid are most beneficial?

  Probe: And what kinds do you feel might cause harm?

  Probe: Would you like to see changes in federal programs? What kinds of changes?

- What do you think the consequences would be if federal funds to state and private higher education were cut off or much reduced?

- In your judgment, does federal money ease the burden of the state or does it simply make it possible for the universities to do things they otherwise would not do?

- Do you think the federal government has a special responsibility in regard to professional training?

- Should federal aid to the different state institutions be channeled through some central state agency?

There is a virtue in taped interviews that other forms of interviews lack. The tape can give a flavor of the respondent's style of thinking and stance that is otherwise highly elusive, yet that gives rich insight into his attitudes and perceptions. We cite four dialogues, not because they are in any way representative, for they are not; but because they exaggerate particular syndromes and are, in their way, "classical" or "ideal-typical" (though, in fact, empirical) demonstrations of different response patterns. We have identified them as those of the "proponent," the "opponent," the "ambivalent," and the "ill-informed." Each of these dialogues speaks for itself.

The Proponent

A Democrat and ranking minority member of a committee in New York:

Interviewer: Do you think the federal government has a special role in the area of professional training?

Respondent: I don't think it has any more special responsibility than it does in the whole area. I think what we need is a balanced federal program, not one of these one-shot deals.

Interviewer: In other words, you don't think that any particular kinds of federal aid are more beneficial?

Respondent: No, I think the federal government should get into the area of education in a massive way and have a balanced program.

Interviewer: Do you foresee any areas in which federal aid might cause trouble?

Respondent: I don't see any problem.

Interviewer: Should federal aid to the various institutions be channeled through some central state agency?

Respondent: Well, that always depends on the system you have in a particular state. In this state, for instance, I am in favor of channeling federal aid for urban areas directly into those areas at other levels—for instance in the area of housing or transportation, although now that has changed because we now have a central transportation authority. But on the higher educational level it would make no sense to make it directly since we have a centrally administered budget. For instance, you could make a separate program for the City University because you have two budget-channeling systems—but you could do that. I don't see any problem in doing it through the State of New York. I think the money would be fairly distributed.

Interviewer: What do you think the consequences would be if federal aid to higher education were cut off or drastically reduced now?

Respondent: I think the consequences would be serious, but not disastrous because we don't have that much aid right now.

Interviewer: Do you foresee a tradeoff here? Does the federal aid reduce the burden on the state, or does it allow the institutions to do things they otherwise couldn't?

Respondent: I think a federal program, for instance, could solve the problem of aid to the private colleges. I really think that the budget squeeze would be on, despite all the glowing things I've said. If we're going to get down to the nitty-gritty of the regent scholarship program, this new regents proposal, which I think is an extremely important proposal, particularly in terms of the urban problem . . . the student coming from a ghetto area is not going to be able to go to college without a subsidy in many, many instances. I mean they are kids who are in the street or are tempted to riot out of frustration—those kids come basically from families who are not going to be able to subsidize a kid for going to school, even if it is free tuition. They can't afford to have a kid going to college. So you've got to have a program in which there are stipends.

The Opponent

A Democrat and chairman of a Texas finance committee:

Interviewer: Some people have suggested that the federal government has a special role to play in providing higher education. What do you think of this view?

Respondent: I don't think that we need them generally, not in Texas.

Interviewer: Speaking of federal aid generally, what is your view of federal aid to higher education?

Respondent: Well, provided that their role is in grants for research, I think that is fine because the research is beneficial to the nation as a whole. But, otherwise, I don't think that they should play such a major role in our institutions of higher education in Texas.

Interviewer: What kind of federal aid would you be opposed to?

Respondent: Any aid that would bring about the desire of the federal government to control higher education, any part of higher education.

Interviewer: Could you be more specific there?

Respondent: Well, if their grant and their aid has strings attached to it, I think that is bad for higher education.

Interviewer: If you could change the role of the federal government, any particular program, or change it in general, in higher education, what changes would you make?

Respondent: Of course, you have to go back to the basic situation. I think you get more for your tax dollar if it doesn't go to Washington and then come back. When the taxes do travel to Washington and back, it is kind of like a poker game with a hole in the middle of the table, and they have a takeoff on the way up and back. So, I am basically of the view that the federal government should leave the money in the states and let the states handle their own money for higher education.

Interviewer: Do you think that the federal aid mainly eases the burdens of the state or that it enables colleges and universities to do things that they could not otherwise do?

Respondent: Neither. I think that if the state was left completely alone about it, they would finance amply and adequately. That is, I think Texas would finance its own higher education program amply and adequately. I think that the Legislature would finance those things which were necessary to be done. I don't know all of the programs that the federal government does finance. But, I doubt if they are all justifiable.

The Ambivalent

A Democratic member of the Texas Senate:

Interviewer: What about the role of the federal government?

Respondent: The federal role is quite controversial around here. Many people tell me that we ought to reject federal aid when it comes. Or that we ought to have aid to higher education now. The truth is that we already have federal aid to higher education, and the question is what is the best role for the use of federal dollars. I think that it can be put to a great deal of good in a great many areas.

Interviewer: Do you have any views as to what kind of federal aid is the most beneficial?

Respondent: Especially, I think facilities aid, aid for medical and professional training and programs of research are the most useful to colleges and universities, but I still think that education, especially higher education, is a state responsibility, that we have not yet reached the state where states are unable to meet their responsibility to higher education. I think, to a large degree, we can meet the needs here without a large number of federal programs.

Interviewer: Does this mean that you would be skeptical of direct grant federal aid programs, say even without strings attached?

Respondent: Well, the answer to that is that there are no federal programs which have no strings attached. What the federal government does is that they come down here and they say that we will give you three-quarters of the funds for this if you will match with one-quarter. Then, the next year, they say that we will put up one half if you will put up the other half. And the next year, they say that they will put up one-quarter if you will put up three-quarters. I think that this is a trap. I think that there is just no federal aid without strings. I think that there will always be some disadvantages of federal aid, and we will just have to realize that higher education is going to have to be a state responsibility.

Interviewer: Suppose because of the Vietnam war, Congress decided that it would have to cut back some domestic programs, in particular, that it would have to cut down on expenditures in higher education. What would the consequences be to higher education?

Respondent: I'd regret it if federal aid were cut off. I would regret it.

The Ill-informed

A Democratic member of an important budget committee in Louisiana:

Interviewer: In general, how do you feel about federal aid to higher education?

Respondent: Well, we don't get any federal aid to higher education in Louisiana, except for buildings, classroom buildings, and so forth.

Interviewer: Do you feel any aspects of the federal program do harm rather than good?

Respondent: I think it could possibly do harm. Whether it has up to now or not, as I said, we actually don't get that; we furnish, we educate our children, but we do get federal aid on buildings. But, I think it could do harm, yes.

Interviewer: Would you suggest any changes in the way the federal program should be conducted?

Respondent: I could suggest a lot of changes in all federal programs, but I don't believe I ought to go into this.

Interviewer: Are you sure?

Respondent: Huh?

Interviewer: Are you sure you just couldn't, just briefly?

Respondent: As far as education?

Interviewer: Just higher education.

Respondent: Not at this time.

To discover the outer limits of legislators' tolerance or intolerance in regard to federal aid for higher education, we asked a question designed to "trap" or commit them—"What do you think the consequences would be if federal funds to the state and private higher education were cut off or much reduced?" How effective this question was is demonstrated by the transcript of a dialogue with an Illinois Democrat:

Interviewer: Do you think the federal government has a special responsibility in regard to professional training?

Respondent: I think we'd all be a little bit better off if the federal goverment was out of higher education.

Interviewer: How do you feel about federal aid to higher education? Do you have any view as to what kinds of federal aid are most beneficial? And what kinds do you feel might cause harm?

Respondent: Most of the money is vested in Title IV and things like that. I think it's a good thing. This federal money has let the school districts and the educators do things that they would not otherwise be able to.

Interviewer: What do you think the consequences would be if federal funds to state and private higher education were cut off or much reduced?

Respondent: Chaotic! Terribly unfortunate, at this time.

Within seconds, this dialogue suggests, the legislator had shifted from feeling that all would be better off "if the federal government was out of higher education" to the judgment that reduction in federal aid would be "chaotic" and "unfortunate" in its consequences.

The question had another unanticipated effect. It seemed to bring out systematic interstate differences that the other questions did not. In general, answer patterns were what one might have expected. Those opposed to federal aid would be likely to write off federal reductions as inconsequential; those favorable to aid would be likely to consider withdrawal of federal aid as disastrous. Yet there was a tendency for respondents in states with less developed higher educational systems, such as Louisiana or Kansas, to show less concern than in the states with more developed systems. The contrast between Louisiana and Texas, for instance, was marked. Not one of the eight Louisiana respondents seemed to consider reduction of federal aid as disastrous.

Legislators in Kansas were more divided, but at least 5 of the 10 respondents were quite sanguine—"There would be quite a shock wave, but I think we would survive"; "It would be quite a strain for a little while, but I think the state certainly would pick up the burden"; "I don't think it would be any great disaster. I think the state could, quite reasonably, pick up the lead very satisfactorily."

By way of contrast, Texans were almost unanimously upset by the prospect of federal withdrawal of support for higher education. The following comment was typical:

It would handicap the problems of all colleges, not only in Texas but in all states. Federal aid at this point is used for construction and research. These two areas would be hurt the most. I imagine that 90 to 95 percent of all federal monies now go into these two basic areas. It would pretty well stop those programs.

Another Texas leader did not accept the probability of federal cuts occurring; in fact, he predicted that the end of the war in Vietnam would see a great expansion of federal aid to education.

A California leader gave a direct and unequivocal response: "We would have to double the budget for the University, right now. . . . The consequences would be very dire if they pulled out flat now." Another Californian, hostile to federal aid, admitted that "it would be, of course, disastrous," but "I'd like to see us do that at the same time we transferred part of the tax dollars back" to the state.

An Iowa Democrat, a committee chairman, differed with those who thought the state would fill the void left by federal cutbacks. He pointed out that the federal government had entered the field in the first place because the states had not been doing the job and that they were unlikely to allocate the needed funds now.

Perhaps the most unbelieving replies came in New York, a state in the midst of building a huge state system of higher education. Replies ranged from "Are you serious?" to "I don't know how the hell they could cut it any more than they have cut it." Evidently New Yorkers were too sophisticated to allow themselves to be trapped by our question.

But at least one response from New York revealed the profound misapprehension that seemed to characterize state legislators' views of the federal government's role in research in all of the states. When even a sophisticated New Yorker, in response to our question about federal cutbacks, replied, "It would hurt, but I don't think it's all that significant. . . . Your federal money, in higher education, it's mostly for research, isn't it?" he betrayed a quite unrealistic, if not uninformed, understanding of the implications of research support for higher education, regardless of whether such support came from federal government, state government, or a private foundation. The impression was strong that few legislators realized that research funds did not just flow into a professor's pockets, but that they were also used for direct and indirect contributions to a number of essential university functions — including the purchase of equipment used in teaching, the financial support of graduate students, and the strengthening of library resources.

TUITION AND FEES   Whether tuition should be increased to pay for the rising costs of higher education was an issue on which state legislators appeared divided. Quite a few agreed with the respondent who favored an increase in tuition because education was available to anyone "if they really work for it." A Texas Representative was emphatic: "It is possible for any boy that really wants to go to school to work to go to school. I don't think anyone is really denied the opportunity to go to school because of lack of funds." And another Texan: "The number one thing of a constructive nature that the Coordinating Board has done is to recommend doubling the tuition in senior colleges. In my opinion, the student ought to pay 25 percent of the cost."

But other respondents said that if there were to be tuition increases, they should be accompanied by more scholarships to take care of needy students. A California legislator remarked:

I'm really very discouraged about the situation, that is, our ability to get more money out of the general treasury into the higher education. I just think we're stuck with some kind of increase in the fee system . . . those who have direct benefit from the program and have the ability are going to have to pay more of the cost of their higher education. And our responsibility then would be to have more scholarships and loans and student-aid programs available to take care of those who do not have the ability to pay.

Another group of legislators felt that tuition should increase as the costs of higher education rose: "Here in Kansas I feel that our tuition rates are necessary and integral parts of the cost sharing of education. And I think they will have to increase as the costs increase."

Perhaps half of our respondents who dealt with the question were opposed to tuition raises. California legislators were the most adamant in opposing tuition.

Out-of-state Tuition   The overwhelming majority of state officials were in favor of higher tuition for out-of-state students than for residents, but not so high that they would be seriously discouraged. Most did not want to *raise* already high tuition. They felt that the exchange of students across state boundaries was beneficial. Kansas legislators, for instance, agreed on (1) not restricting out-of-state admissions and (2) the need for charging out-of-state students more than Kansans. Most of them emphasized that out-of-state students gave the universities an atmosphere of cosmopolitanism and gave local students an opportunity to meet students with different backgrounds and experience.

A Pennsylvanian felt that admissions should not be restricted since some out-of-state students "become Pennsylvania residents and give Pennsylvania the benefit of their expertise and their knowledge." A Senator from Texas suggested that there should be a balance between out-of-state and in-state students, except in areas of pressing need—such as medical and dental schools.

In Kentucky, one of the poorer states, legislators were almost unanimous in feeling that there were too many out-of-state students and that their tuition should be raised. A California legislator said:

I have the impression that the University is admitting too many out-of-state students and is restricting the chances of our own people. I think a lot of the out-of-state students falsify their residential qualifications. I take that back, it may not be dishonesty, but a certain looseness in the regulations. For example, some of the people in my district have complained about militants coming to Berkeley from all over the country, somehow managing to be declared in-state students and paying only local fees.

New York legislators seemed to want to be liberal in admitting out-of-state students but felt priority should be given to their own students. As one stated: "I think that if the admission of an out-of-state student is a deprivation of someone locally, as far as space is concerned, . . . our first obligation is to New York State, unless we have some reciprocity set up with the state of origin."

Efficient Use of Facilities Institutions depending on subsidies rather than profit are invariably suspected of inefficiencies. This is as much the case with government bureaus as it is with schools. Politicians often survive on their criticisms of such institutions. The criticisms make good headlines and may contain an element of truth. We asked our respondents whether there were "ways in which higher education facilities could be used more economically and efficiently." Many felt that the use of classrooms could be more efficient. But, surprisingly, most were more or less satisfied with the ways facilities were used, or did not consider it of major concern.

Criticisms were concerned with the extravagance of the buildings themselves. A Kentucky legislator:

I don't think that it is necessary today for us to put up a fine-looking building that is taller than somebody else's building or possibly has better air-conditioning or has larger rooms or has a little more carpet.

But another Kentuckian explained why some of his colleagues thought money was being wasted:

Part of the reason is that they don't understand how the money is being spent. . . . If you go below the surface of these projects, you usually find that there is a good deal of merit to them.

A Texas representative stated that too many buildings "are going unused for too long a period of time. They're not used at night, on weekends, and through the summer months."

In Iowa, New York, and Kansas most legislators felt that the use of buildings in the summer was the best way to make more efficient use of equipment. It was felt that this would enable the size of the classes to be reduced. Trimester plans and night classes were also suggested to reduce the numbers of classes and make more efficient use of facilities. A legislator from New York was not sure, however, that small classes were necessary. He thought that higher education institutions "could probably handle more people more efficiently through the use of new techniques now available—educational TV, teaching machines, and the exposure of large groups to good teachers. Some dramatic change in the teacher-student ratio might be indicated."

TAXPAYERS' WILLINGNESS TO PAY Few of our questions elicited as lively responses as this one: "How willing would you say are the taxpayers in (state) to support higher education?"

The question, it seems, fascinates politicians not only because their political survival depends on keeping taxpayers content but also because in this respect, at least, they can be as "representative" as it is possible to be under modern conditions of democracy.

While most respondents thought taxpayers were willing to support higher education, quite a few felt there was some reluctance or even unwillingness. The reasons included recent unrest on campuses, already high taxes, an opposition to "luxury" spending on campuses, and ignorance of the real problems of higher education. A number of legislators said that the people were unaware of how the money was divided up and that they were not specifically antagonistic to higher education, but rather to taxes and spending in general.

Nonetheless, the majority of legislators believed that taxpayers were prepared to foot the bill for higher education. Common reasons given were public pride, the way in which higher education was financed, the fact that educators from the colleges and universities did a good job of selling, and public awareness of the need for higher education.

Several leaders perceived the public as resenting taxes in general, rather than as reluctant to support higher education. The chairman of a Senate appropriations and revenue committee said people were unhappy with a recently instituted sales tax:

I think basically the taxpayers are willing to pay what they feel is the reasonable and necessary expense of government, including the expense of educating the children. I think they have the distinct impression at the present time that the five-cent sales tax was not necessary, that a four-cent sales tax would do the job.

A member of the Committee on Higher Education in Illinois thought that the people were dissatisfied with the revenue procedures:

They're willing, very willing [to support higher education]. Some junior college bonds are defeated because the people are dissatisfied with the archaic revenue procedures used in Illinois. You know, it's a property tax; it's a very ancient procedure.

A Pennsylvania chairman made a similar comment and a legislator from Iowa saw no reluctance on the part of average taxpayers to pay for higher education as long as the money was spent wisely.

In California, only two legislators doubted the taxpayers' continuing willingness to finance public higher education. One of these thought that there ought to be a better dialogue between the public and political leadership and detected an increasing unwillingness to pay for public projects:

I think the changing economic value system in our society over the past 20 years has deemphasized the willingness of people to spend on public things. This disturbs me a great deal. I think it's due possibly to the fact that we are a fluid society, and that television has raised people's personal and private desires, and so I think public education is going to have to compete under less favorable circumstance if this trend continues.

The chairman of a committee on education in New York mentioned dislike for taxes, but thought that people realized the importance of higher education. Another Assemblyman from New York was more cynical: "Oh yes. Education is one of the sacred cows of our modern governmental era. The general education lobbyists are very active and good."

Several legislators who mentioned an unwillingness of taxpayers to pay for higher education felt that the public was perhaps ignorant of the problems. The chairman of a senate committee on higher education said the legislators in his state were more aware than the people of the problems stemming from an increasing student population. A legislator from Iowa thought that the people's ignorance was in part due to the fact that so much of Iowa's population was over 65.

A number of legislators attributed taxpayers' reluctance to finance higher education to concern over campus radicalism and disruption. A Texas Representative said: "The general public doesn't want the kind of . . . educational environment which creates a Berkeley or a University of Chicago. That is offensive to the average taxpayer." A member of the Iowa House also thought that taxpayers were disturbed about campus radicalism, specifically "recent incidents at the institutions led by the hippies and demonstrations, pot, LSD, and marijuana at Iowa State." A California legislator, though he thought taxpayers were basically supportive of higher education, felt that this support was being undermined by radical activities.

DILEMMAS OF THE PRIVATE INSTITUTIONS Private colleges and universities have traditionally played a vital role in higher education. Until recently they have educated the majority of college students in this country, and many of them are recognized for the quality of their graduate and undergraduate training. Their contribution to education, however, is clearly being challenged. In 1957 the ratio of public to private students was 1.37 to 1; by 1967 it had risen to 2.11 to 1, and it is estimated to reach 2.75 to 1 by 1977 (U.S. Department of Health, Education, and Welfare, 1969, p. 16). In part these figures represent the substantial increase in the proportion of college-age persons now attending institutions of higher education. In part, too, they represent the increasing financial problems which many of the private colleges and universities are experiencing. In the face of rapidly rising costs, virtually all private schools are raising tuition at unprecedented rates. In 1957 the average tuition charged by private institutions was $684; in 1967 it was $1,327. Tuition and fees at public schools during this period rose on an average from $182 to $292.

Despite additional income from tuition, however, the financial future of private schools is not bright. In a recent survey of 20 of the more prestigious private colleges and universities, it was found that they would have a combined operating deficit of $3 million in 1968; by 1973 it was estimated that they would probably exhaust their reserves and run up a deficit of $45 million (Norton-Taylor, 1967, p. 153). Thus private institutions will be hard pressed to maintain their traditional role. Many of the smaller and/or less prestigious schools are likely to face bankruptcy; others may be forced to limit their enrollment to the well-to-do. Without some additional means of outside funding, the future of private colleges and universities does not look promising.

The state legislators and officials were asked about their perceptions of the role of private education in their states, how the states might assist these schools, and how private schools were likely to fare in the future. Their answers were highly varied. While almost all had a positive assessment of private education, their perceptions of the problems facing private schools and how the state should respond were more hetereogeneous. In general, the legislators and executives were not particularly disturbed about the financial plight of the private schools. When pressed, most replied that these schools were valuable assets to the state and that the legislature should do what it could to help them. However, the majority of state officials did not support direct financial assistance to private institutions but would limit the state's role to providing individual scholarship aid. Their reasons were many— including disbelief in the financial burdens of private schools, constitutional limitations, and other financial priorities. Probably the major reason given was the fear that direct state assistance would inevitably result in state control of some sort. Such control, many thought, would undermine the traditional qualities and independence of private education.

Unlike many other areas of the survey, consistent state patterns of response emerged here. State leaders in New York, Pennsylvania, and Iowa were generally more concerned about the financial problems of private schools and more receptive to some type of direct state assistance. Not coincidentally, private schools educated a larger proportion of students in these states than in others included in the survey. In New York and Pennsylvania the majority of college students were enrolled in private colleges or universities, while about 40 percent of Iowa's college population attended such schools. In California, Kansas, and Louisiana, by contrast, less than one-fifth of college students received a private education.

CONCLUSION On the whole, legislators in the nine states were supportive of higher education. They were reasonably sensitive to the variety of problems facing their public institutions. However, one got the feeling that even the best-informed and most intelligent among them had at times only vague notions of the complexities of university finance. Their reactions to problems, their perceptions of priorities, their suggestions for remedies, or their understanding of popular reactions were often superficial and, in some cases, highly stereotypic. Those critical of higher education often responded to particular incidents or experiences. But all, it seemed, were seriously concerned with the problem of financing the public institutions, for appropriations are in fact the most direct concern of legislative decision makers. Some were more optimistic than others that the financial problems could be solved, depending largely on their state's tax structure and the realistic options available. Most of them were incrementalists—they were aware of the constraints under which budgets must be made. And few seemed to feel a need for the injection of massive new funds. Even those we interviewed, all of whom were more or less directly involved in financing higher education, either as members of relevant committees or as leaders, were sensitive to the fact that higher education was, after all, only one area of state activities that required their attention.

6. Legislators and Academicians

The faculty are an integral part of higher education. They provide the majority of teaching instruction, serve as formal and informal counselors to students, and share in the governing of educational institutions. Colleges and universities are judged primarily upon the quality of their faculties. Yet, although money may attract highly qualified individuals, a large budget cannot in itself guarantee that a school will become a leader in the educational field. How a state goes about recruiting and retaining faculty is thus of utmost importance to the fulfillment of its educational goals.

State legislatures, of course, play a crucial role in this process. Through the allocation of state funds, they are able to determine—directly or indirectly—the level of faculty salaries in their states and the amount of money available for such additional attractions as research and graduate studies. Through their ability to pass legislation regulating faculty and student conduct, they are in a position to influence the academic atmosphere and attractiveness of state colleges and universities. A hostile legislature which requires loyalty oaths, investigates campus affairs, and brings political pressures to bear upon trustees and administrators can be as much of a handicap in attracting faculty as low salary schedules.

There are, it would appear, a number of reasons to expect conflict between legislators and faculty members. In the first place, legislators must allocate funds for a variety of state agencies and employees. Since higher education accounts for a large proportion of the states' nondedicated funds, state officials are likely to be more concerned with questions of economy and efficiency than are academicians. Secondly, state legislators are directly accountable to the electorate, a burden which college professors do not share. The electorate is frequently more critical of higher education than state officials—who are themselves predominantly college educated

—and often exerts strong pressures upon them to regulate university affairs. Campus unrest, as will be seen in Chapter 8, is one area in which the public is apparently more critical than are state officials, and more supportive of punitive legislation. Faculty members themselves, finally, are primarily responsive to and regulated by professional norms and rewards. Few laymen can be expected to appreciate the need for academic research and publication; fewer still the extent to which academic success is judged on these grounds. To the outsider, the primary task of the professor is likely to be seen as providing classroom instruction, not as establishing a professional reputation.

Thus a great potential for conflict exists between state legislators and the faculty of state colleges and universities. The former are responsive to what they consider their states' needs—education being only one—and are highly susceptible to public pressures. Faculty are responsive primarily to their profession and to their colleagues. When state legislators exercise their authority over faculty members, they are likely to do so on the basis of a different set of perceptions and a different set of priorities. State leaders' perceptions of four such areas of potential conflict—attracting and retaining faculty, faculty salaries, faculty work loads, and faculty participation in public affairs—are the subject of this chapter. As will be seen, the opinions of state legislators and executives are indeed different from those commonly expressed by academic personnel.

ATTRACTING AND RETAINING FACULTY Most state leaders indicated a high degree of pride and satisfaction in their own faculties. The majority of legislators reported that their states were doing an excellent job of attracting and retaining faculty and would do so in the future. Typical of their replies were:

Yes, I think we do [retain a good faculty], and we underpay them a little bit. And considering that fact, I think we do a remarkably good job of retaining them. We have a lot of dedicated faculty.

Frankly, I am amazed how well we have done when you consider our faculty salaries, how near on the fringe we have been. I am amazed how well we have done.

If we consider the doctor's degree any gauge at all in comparing the institutions in Texas with those in Louisiana, Oklahoma, Arkansas, right on across the East Coast, I don't recall more than two or three universities and colleges who have higher standards of instructors than we have right here in Texas.

The most notable expressions of dissatisfaction were found among the California respondents—a number of whom felt that the state's ability to attract good professors had declined. Several doubted whether California was doing as well as it should or as well as it had in the past. As one official pointed out: "Other states are recruiting in California now. . . . Very few people were previously recruiting in California because no one left the state." The principal reasons cited for California's declining position were (1) that faculty salaries were no longer sufficiently competitive with other states, (2) that campus disruptions and attacks by the state administration upon campus autonomy had made California less attractive to first-rate professors, and (3) that the emphasis on publication as a prerequisite for advancement had been carried too far in the state.

Although legislators sometimes disagreed among themselves on how well their respective states were faring in academic competition, most felt that high salaries were the most important single factor in their relative success or lack of it. A number of officials said their states were more successful in recruiting faculty than they had been in the past because of salary increases. Such a position, for example, was taken by a number of Louisiana respondents. Others felt that their states were losing out because of their low salary levels. "There is a shortage of top-grade instructors," an Iowa legislator asserted. "You've got to raise salaries and appropriations to keep people." A Kansas official similarly thought that his state was having difficulty retaining faculty because of its low salaries:

It's very difficult to retain individuals in the state because of salary. The competition is very great for academic personnel. . . . If we're going to get some of these better people—and I don't think publishing is necessarily a criterion for better people—I think we're going to have to pay more money.

Most other factors were considered as secondary to salaries. Many officials felt that there was little the state could do to reduce faculty mobility; faculty members achieved professional recognition, they pointed out, by moving from school to school. Additional factors mentioned included research opportunities, tenure policies, an overemphasis upon research, and the academic environment of a state. Of these probably the last was the most important. A Texan explained what he thought was his state's relative lack of success in retaining faculty:

We are not maintaining the academic environment in the state that we ought to be. We are not encouraging freedom of expression on the part of our faculty members. We are imposing too many restrictions and regulations on what an individual faculty member can do or say. . . . I think that he ought to be judged as a teacher and as a scholar rather than on his political opinions. And I think that we judge very strongly. We judge our faculty at our Texas universities a great deal on what they seem to think and the political nature of what they are teaching.

THE ISSUE OF FACULTY SALARIES As noted, most respondents regarded high, competitive salaries as the most crucial factor in attracting and retaining faculty. When asked if faculty salaries in their states were adequate, however, they were far from unanimous in their opinions. They were about evenly divided between those who thought salaries were adequate, or even too high, and those who thought they were not adequate or might be too low. Several legislators were ambivalent, failing to commit themselves one way or the other.

The respondents generally seemed to evaluate the "adequacy" of faculty salaries in their respective states in light of two criteria: First, were salaries competitive with those of other states and with industry and other professions? Were they high enough to attract and to retain the caliber of faculty the state needed? Second, were the faculty getting the amount of pay they deserved? Were they adequately paid for the amount of time and effort they put into teaching?

The variation in responses depended largely upon whether the legislators felt their states' salaries were sufficiently competitive and whether they felt the state was getting its money's worth. As will be seen below, many respondents wanted faculty members to spend a greater proportion of their time in the classroom.

Respondents in New York, Pennsylvania, Texas, and California were most likely to report that faculty salaries were too low. "Some professors are making pretty good money these days," a Pennsylvania legislator asserts, "but the pay isn't uniform and perhaps it should be increased." A New York official replied simply, "We've got to make up our minds that we have to pay these people enough to attract qualified people." Texans, eager to achieve a first-rate system of higher education, also tended to view salaries as too low. Two Texas legislators specified higher faculty salaries as the "number one" need in their state. As noted in the previous section, Californians were most likely to be dissatisfied with faculty salaries. Many felt that salary levels were primarily responsible for the state's recent inability to retain or attract top faculty—particularly in competition with New York. Several officials also complained about the salary differences between the state colleges and universities; salaries at the former, they thought, were too low. "After visiting the campuses," one legislator answered, "I have no question in my mind that recruiting is difficult because our salaries now are not competitive, apparently, with many other comparable or even lesser institutions."

About an equal number of respondents thought faculty salaries were adequate or too high. Most of these respondents pointed out that the faculty received many fringe benefits in addition to their salaries and frequently obtained outside income from research grants, publications, and consultation. "They are all doing consulting for one or another foundation or business or something else," one official responded, "and as a consequence I don't attach that much significance to salaries per se." An Iowa Senator said:

Well, compared to other salaries in the Iowa economy and in the national economy, I think the faculties in our state institutions are doing quite well. The public isn't aware . . . and other government authorities in Iowa aren't aware of some of the benefits . . . you people on the faculty enjoy. . . . By and large, I think, for the hours spent, you're pretty well paid when you consider the fringe benefits. Many of you do outside research work in one thing or another.

"It's a pretty nice life in many ways," he concluded. "Nice atmosphere, a lot of cultural advantages, and so on." A New York legislator also thought that additional compensation was readily available to the resourceful faculty member:

Well, as I see it, and again this I don't know in depth, but as I see it, any resourceful academician today can make a very good livelihood in academic life. I think we are paying a fairly good base . . . there is such a tremendous opportunity now beyond income from the universities themselves in the very thing that you are doing, the study commission, the innumerable study commissions.

A California legislator called the University "derelict" in its presentation of salary figures to the Legislature:

I think the University has been derelict in the matter of free disclosure of information to the Ways and Means Committee and the Assembly. They have always given us the impression that faculty salaries are too low. But they never take into account—at least they don't tell us—about the outside income of faculty members. Most of you guys are going off in all directions making money.

Faculty members, he charged, were "using the best tax-supported higher education facilities in the country" for their private use. "You're not teaching the kids well enough," he told his academic interviewer. "You're not around for talking to them, but you can use your offices and your libraries and your labs to make all kinds of money."

Whether or not they thought faculty salaries adequate, most respondents felt they would continue to increase. Such increases, most believed, would be necessary if their states were to remain competitive and if faculty salaries were to keep up with the cost of living. At least two legislators, however, were critical of the procedure by which faculty members bargained for higher salaries. The most outspoken of the two, a California Senator, called the process the "greatest and most fascinating conspiracy in combination in the restraint of trade that has ever come upon the face of the earth":

Salaries in California may be too low in competition with salaries in New York, which got high because of New York, which boosted salaries in California. . . . If that little game of playing both ends against the middle hadn't gotten so far ahead, faculty salaries might not be twice what would [normally] be needed to pick the top men.

An Illinois Assemblyman described the process similarly but was less disturbed by it:

The method that's used in the education field . . . is . . . if they get a pay increase in Illinois, they wire their brothers in Lansing and say,

"Look, we got a pay increase." Then they say, "Hey, Illinois is way above our standards" . . . and everybody plays leapfrog.

"Of course," he continued, "teachers have been in great demand, and if you believe in free enterprise as I do, it seems to me that you have to believe that we should meet the going market price for them."

THE ISSUE OF FACULTY WORK LOAD "Well, of course, everybody feels that they don't work hard enough." A New York Assemblyman spoke for many respondents when he made this statement. When asked how they felt about faculty work loads, the majority of state officials replied that they were too low; most felt that college professors led "a pretty soft life." The rare legislators who replied that faculty members were overburdened were often themselves present or former members of the academic community.

Typically, legislators asserted that faculty had a great deal of assistance in their teaching duties and apparently had a large amount of time to pursue their "own affairs." Many officials equated teaching hours with work hours, and few regarded research as a part of the college professor's required duties. Representative answers to this question were:

To my knowledge—and from the information I have—I don't think that very many of them are overworked.

From what I know about it, I think that their work load is about right because they have assistants to do most of their work—assistants, clerks, or whatever you want to call them.

I think we're doing a fair job here. I don't think that any of them are complaining too severely about work load or extra work assigned to them. At least it has not come to my attention.

I don't hear a lot of complaints from my sources in the faculty locker room. At least they still have time to get over and play ball and squash. . . . Even the ones who want to publish seem to have time to do this.

It was clear that most state officials considered the proper role of the faculty members to be that of "teacher" or "counselor." The majority did not feel that research was a legitimate or desirable part of the role. Few had any idea that publication was often a requirement of tenure. The most frequently voiced criticism of faculty members was that they were spending too much time in "personal" or "outside" activities—by which the respondents meant research endeavors—and too little time in the classroom. A California official said that such an image of faculty members was the predominant one among legislators. A second Californian indicated that the typical legislative evaluation of the faculty work load was that it was "lax." If it weren't, he reasoned, professors could not be "out leading demonstrations." He went on to voice another frequently heard complaint: "In general, legislators don't like the high number of teaching assistants that are used, instead of students facing bona fide faculty persons."

Such remarks about the use of graduate students as teaching assistants were frequent. A Kansas legislator pointed out that from his own experience in college, the "actual teaching frequently is not done by the professor. . . . The job is given to some graduate student, while [the professor] does research or goes out on some advisory project." A second official said:

I think the work load is too low. I really do, and I think we've gone overboard in what teaching loads we've let them pressure us into believing that they ought to have. . . . My inclination is that as soon as those people finish a class, they're off that campus as fast as they can go and back home writing a book or doing some research or something else. Or carrying on some other moonlighting job.

A number of respondents felt that some way should be found to reward those engaged in teaching more than they presently are. "They should be paid enough money," as one official asserted, "to keep them in the classrooms." A California Assemblyman asserted that he spoke for the entire legislature in his state in arguing that "good teachers"—those who spend their time in the classroom rather than doing research—should be better rewarded. A Kansas legislator made a similar distinction between "working teachers" and "professors." The former, he thought, were not adequately paid.

Not surprisingly, legislators with academic backgrounds tended to be less critical. Many of the state leaders who indicated that faculty work loads were high had themselves been faculty members. Among these was a Kansas legislator who served on the faculty of a junior college. He claimed that the faculty worked harder than most legislators realized and that teaching involved much more than the number of hours spent in front of a class:

My brother teaches mathematics . . . and . . . he seems to think . . . that a 9- or a 12-hour load is a pretty good load when you have a lot of preparations in higher mathematics. . . . I know at . . . the graduate level, we are expected to do more research. You are committed to reading more term papers and giving guidance to students on research projects. . . . Really when you're talking about a 12-hour work load, you're just talking about part of your job that you have in teaching.

A California legislator, a former college teacher with many contacts at the University of California, said:

I think the state colleges will find it more and more difficult to compete with institutions of higher education in other states which are comparable because in California the state college teaching load is pretty high. But the members of the Legislature here, I'm convinced, are not of that opinion at all, and I think they believe that state college faculty should spend more time in the classrooms. . . . They are not disposed to a program of research, even limited research.

The most sympathetic response came from a New York legislator who advocated that faculty be "given a lot more credit than they are given." He felt they should have sufficient time to do independent research and said, "If the individual faculty member is so loaded down that he has no time for research, something is wrong."

FACULTY PARTICIPATION IN PUBLIC AFFAIRS "What is your opinion about faculty participation in public affairs?" the respondents were asked. "Should they participate or stay out?"

They invariably replied that faculty members should become involved in public affairs. The faculty, they asserted, are citizens and, like every citizen, have the right and duty to participate. A number of respondents went even further and declared that faculty members—by virtue of their superior education and intelligence—have a particular duty to contribute to society through public involvement.

At issue in these responses, as might be expected, was the officials' definition of "public affairs." Far from advocating that professors be political activists, most legislators defined the proper public role of faculty members in narrow, conventional terms. Participation in such activities as civic clubs, Boy Scout and Girl

Scout troops, the Red Cross, service clubs, and the chamber of commerce were strongly urged. Participation in antiwar activities, radical organizations, and often even partisan campaigns was discouraged. State leaders, in other words, would largely limit the role of faculty members to social-service organizations. Very few were willing to tolerate, much less encourage, faculty participation in unconventional activities. Many indicated that it was proper for college professors to engage in partisan politics, but those who approved of such practices frequently cautioned the faculty to be careful not to associate their university with their private activities.

A typical response was that of a Texas Senator. "I think that they ought to be allowed to participate just like any other citizen," he declared. "Just because they are faculty, you shouldn't put a muzzle on them. They are citizens." A New York legislator took a similar position: "I am definitely opposed to the idea of their staying out. I don't think they should be any different than anyone else. Whether they are professors or workingmen, they should participate." Others emphasized the "responsibility" of faculty members to engage in such activities by virtue of their positions as educators. "They're deeply involved in public affairs by being in there," a California Assemblyman asserted, "and by not taking an active part, then I think they're evading their responsibility." A Kentucky Senator admitted that "some faculty members . . . say things I wish they wouldn't." But, he continued, "they'd better participate in the public affairs because, after all, they are part of the brainpower in the state."

An Illinois legislator asserted:

They should participate in many more areas than they do. I think that the faculty have a unique contribution that they could make, and many of them are not doing it. . . . If they would take a much more active part in the Rotary and Kiwanis and Lions and other areas—chamber of commerce, junior chamber of commerce, and so forth—the people downtown would see that they really were human.

A Texas legislator thought that college professors should become actively involved in civic affairs so as to upgrade the community. An Iowa Assemblyman differentiated between involvement in peace rallies and Boy Scout and Girl Scout troops, condemning the former and endorsing the latter:

I'm of the strong opinion that they must become involved because, by nature, they are knowledgeable people. . . . Because of this, they have a leadership role and should exercise that in public affairs. Unfortunately, the . . . ones that we hear about are those who make the headlines because of peace rallies and so forth. This is not the type of involvement that I refer to. . . . We have professors who serve as advisers to Boy Scout troops and Girl Scout troops and so forth.

Not all state officials would limit the faculty's role in public affairs to participation in civic clubs or organizations. A large number, probably the majority of the respondents, would allow them to participate in partisan politics as well. A few legislators criticized college professors for their naive and arrogant attitudes toward politics and the political process and advocated that they should become engaged in partisan politics to "find out what it was really like." A New York Assemblyman argued that educators did not know enough about politics and suggested that they obtain an education by running for public office. "I think it would be an eye-opener for some of them," he asserted. "I think they have no conception, really, of . . . public office."

A New York Senator was especially critical. There was, he felt, a great deal of snobbery among academicians about the political process. He went on to argue that one must know how to solve problems practically as well as intellectually or theoretically. A California Senator said:

You know, the thing that really amuses me, the very guy who sits down there before 30, 40, 50, a hundred kids and talks about political science has a tremendous contempt for the system. And I think this is bad. Because his very existence, his very freedom, depends on legislation or lack of it. And here he has a tremendous contempt; he ridicules politics and politicians all through his lectures. He is so far removed from the reality of life politically that to me it is just fantastic.

A Kansas legislator approved of partisan activities but said college professors should not "run for public office on the state's time." A Texas official said:

I favor participation if they want to. I don't think they should be forced to. I think that if they are able to divorce themselves from their educational institutions and participate in public affairs on an individual basis, there should be no basic restrictions.

A New York Assemblyman took a similar position:

As individuals, I think they certainly have the right to. I think they have an obligation, as far as they can, to divorce themselves from projecting the image that this is the faculty position or that it is the university position. I guess I have a negative reaction to the State University faculty committee on this or that when it is getting out of the educational field.

Many respondents, as might be expected, condemned faculty involvement in radical or militant activities. The more conservative legislators frequently included college professors in their denunciation of student activism, while others argued that faculty members were hurting their own institutions by engaging in certain forms of behavior. A California official probably spoke for many when he asserted:

When they get involved with the militants, when they get in with the agitators, they tear down their image. I think that now all professors are suspect by the people, even the good ones. People are losing their confidence in the University.

While none of the respondents suggested that legislation should be passed restricting the activities of professors, it was clear that the majority were critical of militant faculty behavior. The reaction of public officials to faculty activism was thus similar to their reaction toward student activism: they strongly disapproved of the conduct but did not want to involve the legislature in the situation.

CONCLUSION   It is apparent that state officials' perceptions of faculty members are highly colored by their own positions and that their views are frequently in conflict with the prevailing opinion of academia. Most state leaders exhibited a good deal of pride in their own faculties and anticipated that their states would attract competent faculty personnel in the future. The only major exception was in California where a number of respondents believed that their state was losing its competitive edge. At the same time the state officials were split on the question of salaries. About half thought they were adequate or too high, about half that they were too low. Regardless of their position on this question, however, almost all respondents said that faculty salaries were the major means to attract top personnel and that they would go up in the future.

The contrasting perceptions of public officials and college professors were most apparent on the issues of faculty work load and involvement in public affairs. Few legislators or executives considered research to be a necessary part of the academic role. Most thought that faculty should spend most or all of their time in the classroom, and many equated work load with classroom teaching hours. Almost all state leaders, as a result, felt that the faculty work load was too low; they considered research and publication to be a part of the professor's "outside" or "personal" activities. Many of those who argued that the faculty were well compensated pointed to the additional funds which they often received for these outside activities.

Faculty participation in public affairs was favored by most officials. It was apparent from their responses, however, that their definition of public affairs was a limited one. Many urged the faculty to become more active in civic and community organizations. Those who approved of their participation in partisan politics often asserted that they should divorce themselves from the university in doing so. None supported faculty involvement in radical or militant activities. No direct question was asked on this last issue, but many officials volunteered their views on the matter anyway.

7. The Junior College Phenomenon

Junior colleges are the fastest growing public institutions of higher education in the country. During the past decade, their enrollments have multiplied 2½ times—a growth rate almost twice that of four-year colleges. In most parts of the country junior colleges have clearly been adopted as a major mechanism to meet the increasing demands for higher education. Some states have excelled in this respect. California is generally recognized as possessing one of the finest and most developed junior college systems in the country; others, such as Kansas, are just beginning to coordinate their efforts. All states, however, are placing more and more resources into two-year colleges and are using them to educate greater numbers of students.

The popularity of junior colleges was clearly reflected in the responses of state legislators and executive officials. They were more positive in their evaluations of these colleges than of any other aspect of higher education covered in the survey. All but a handful of state officials said that the growth of junior colleges had had beneficial effects upon education in their states, and most saw an even greater role and expansion in the future. The only major criticism pertained to the coordination of these rapidly expanding institutions. A number of legislators thought the junior colleges had been developed in such haste and for such a variety of purposes that it was necessary to define more carefully their role in the state's educational plans and to coordinate their activities and growth with those of the four-year institutions. Such criticisms were made, however, not in the desire to curtail junior colleges but to make them more effective.

From the interviews it appeared that a major reason for the widespread acceptance and approval of junior colleges by state officials was that they fulfilled such a wide variety of functions. Economy-minded legislators generally regarded the junior colleges as less expensive than their four-year equivalents. Those who thought that greater efforts should be made to assist the less advantaged student approved of them because they were much cheaper and more accessible to students. Those who were often less supportive of higher education liked them because they provided technical and vocational training and served to attract industry.

The spread of junior colleges seems to have been assisted also by the political nature of their construction. Local communities, it was reported, saw the possession of a junior college as a source of prestige and a means to attract residents and wealth. Although such factors were generally mentioned with disapproval, it was apparent that politics had played a substantial role in the expansion of the junior college system in many states.

THE MULTIPLE FUNCTIONS OF THE JUNIOR COLLEGE

Most state officials said junior colleges were an important element in meeting the demands placed upon higher education within their respective states. The manner in which these institutions were to carry out such a role, however, varied greatly. Some respondents saw junior colleges as academic, liberal arts-oriented schools from which sophomores could transfer to four-year institutions; some as a vocational training center for those young persons who did not have the ability or interest to pursue further college education. Still others spoke of the college's general service to the local community. Many legislators, of course, mentioned two or more of these functions.

The problem of defining the role of junior colleges was, in fact, central to the responses of many state leaders — particularly in those states which were just beginning to develop their own systems. A Kansas official, for example, said:

The junior college question in Kansas is one that has not been resolved. Some hard looks need to be taken to see what we are doing and what kind of structure we are creating and the relationship with the other state institutions. . . . Are we talking about comprehensive community colleges at the two-year level with some transferability of credit? . . . Are they going to be in fact an extension of higher education, or are they going to, as they do now, offer part vocational? . . . These questions are relatively unsolved.

A second Kansan admitted confusion over this problem: "The role of the junior college has not been clearly established," he asserted, "and I am not sure in my own mind what the role is. I thought I knew, but I become more confused when I talk to the junior college people really." Still a third Kansas official said:

We have to redefine the role of the junior colleges. Are they going to be a glorified vocational school, or are they really going to be a preparatory school between high school and the college level? I don't think the state can afford to have the mixture of both as it is existing today. We need to decide on one or the other function. Vocational training is one of the areas we need to meet. Now if the junior colleges want to go academic, then let's go that way. If they are going to go vocational-technical as they are and mix it in . . . I think a redefinition of their goals and all should be made.

The majority, however, took a quite different point of view and advocated that the junior colleges continue to play a multiplicity of roles. The most explicit in this respect was the following respondent:

I think that they can offer the first two years of college work at a level which is satisfactory for academic transfer into your junior or senior year. I'm not saying that all of them are doing this. I think they can serve the purpose of providing terminal types of education and technical types of education. I'm sold on the concept that there can be a multipurpose type of institution and have all of these under one roof.

Many legislators would place greater emphasis upon certain aspects of junior college training, but few would limit the roles of these institutions. Roles most frequently mentioned were liberal arts training, vocational-technical training, and service to the local community.

Liberal Arts Training   The majority of state officials felt that the junior colleges should serve at least partially as liberal arts institutions—providing the student with a terminal education or preparing him for further training in a four-year college or university. While both functions were mentioned by large numbers of legislators, the emphasis was generally placed on the "screening" rather than the "feeding" role of junior colleges. A Kentucky legislator was typical: "I think . . . the community college is a very excellent screener of students. I think a person can actually go to a community college and perhaps determine whether he is a fit candidate say for the third and fourth academic years."

The screening function of the junior colleges was seen as advantageous to the student, to state budgets, and to the educational system itself. Several leaders suggested that if the junior colleges were used to "weed out" non-college material, it would relieve some of the pressure on the four-year schools, saving money for both the students and the state. Such a position was taken by a Louisiana Senator:

All students are not, of course, college material . . . some of them, their talents lie in other directions, such as a trade school. Well, they could find that out at a junior college or at a commuter college at very little cost to the student or the state.

An Illinois Republican:

The junior colleges provide a very much more effective and cheaper way of doing this initial screening rather than having all the students go, say, to the state university and having most of them flunked out after a semester or two.

And a Louisiana official:

We've got a preponderant number of people here in rural areas, as well as metropolitan areas, who, it seems to me, just simply aren't college material. It seems to me therefore that we are expending a great deal of our effort and our money in trying to put over these massive programs to educate the uneducatable. . . . I believe we have literally thousands of kids who would be happier and who would serve society better if they were able to get a couple of years of junior college background and then go into some vocational field . . . and from that standpoint I think that our whole educational system beyond high school would be on a better base.

Although most of those who spoke of the screening function of the junior colleges seemed to view the process largely in terms of weeding out unqualified students, others characterized it in more positive terms. Among them was the Pennsylvania state Representative who thought the junior colleges should serve as "feeders" from which qualified students would go on to "take the third and fourth years of college and then go on to graduate school." A New York administrator similarly argued that the opportunity for service in many of our four-year institutions could be greater if they concentrated on the upper-division and graduate-level work, at least in some of the institutions.

Vocational-technical Training

The majority of respondents—even those who thought that the junior colleges should perform many roles—indicated that particular emphasis would or should be given to vocational-technical training and two-year terminal education programs. The following response of a Texas legislator was typical of those who saw the vocational role as primary:

> Part of the junior college curriculum is a step to senior college education, and part of it is and should be vocational training, where you don't need a senior college education. But the technical and vocational training are the point of emphasis in my opinion in the junior colleges.

More commonly, legislators indicated that vocational training should simply be emphasized along with the other functions performed by the junior colleges. Thus a New York official felt that junior colleges "naturally" would place heavy emphasis on vocational-technical programs and "would be offering terminal education to a great many," but would not limit their role to this area. Another New Yorker agreed on the priority of vocational-technical education but disagreed on how well this was actually working in his state:

Interviewer: What do you see as the virtues of the junior colleges?

Respondent: They . . . take on the latebloomers and the vocational education people, with a kind of secondary emphasis on transfer students. . . . [This is] very beneficial, especially vocational education. I think it's very important.

Interviewer: Do you think this is working out well?

Respondent: No I don't. Not at all. I think that they're almost as much involved in the university syndrome as the state colleges are. They want to be four-year colleges. . . . No, I don't think it's working well at all.

Almost all of our respondents thought that vocational training programs and "practical" education were being neglected in their states and looked to the junior colleges as a means of remedying the deficiency. Some of these leaders seemed to feel that the junior colleges should specialize almost exclusively in vocational-technical training and let the four-year schools handle "academic" education. The junior colleges, a New York legislator said, "are best equipped to conduct the semiprofessional programs which are burgeoning in the health fields and technical fields and so on . . . you can't see a four-year college doing this." Another New Yorker would use vocational education as a means to shorten the industrial training period.

How many people can come out of college with an A.B. and do anything useful? That is except for teachers. You know the training they are getting for the A.B. now is about equivalent to the meaning of a high school degree a few years ago. They are not much use for employers. I think if we can train more people in vocational education, we can shorten the training time that industry itself finds necessary, and we could get higher starting salaries for people.

An Iowa chairman agreed. In his opinion, the virtue of the junior colleges was that they "meet the need of the person who is either not fitted for or doesn't desire an academic education, who is just leaving high school and going to work some place."

Service to the Community A final function which many legislators suggested the junior colleges should perform could perhaps best be characterized as "service to the community." In addition to training technically skilled personnel—and thus aiding local business and attracting new industry—the junior college was cast in the role of providing nondegree programs to local citizens. Some leaders felt that the high schools were failing to teach people the basic skills and knowledge needed to live in a rapidly changing society and that the junior colleges could help by offering remedial courses. A California Assemblyman said:

I think they should be dealing with basic educational things since the high schools are falling down. I think they have to teach people how to speak, how to type, [how] to understand the English language. I don't want the junior colleges to have big ideas about academic programs. They have to prepare their people for life.

Other legislators suggested that junior colleges should provide continuing education for adults who were not interested in getting a college degree, but who wanted to broaden the scope of their knowledge or to pursue an interest in a particular subject. A Kentucky leader said: "You might offer a course in the stock market . . . or landscape gardening . . . or a course in tailoring for the ladies. I think this is a very important part of the education process."

A California Democrat expressed the views of many state leaders when he declared, "The virtues of the junior colleges are a great many," and noted especially "the ongoing opportunity for anyone living in the community to extend his education to broader areas, no matter what kind of a degree he may have." There are, he pointed out, "courses available day and night that he may wish to take to broaden his knowledge."

THE PERCEIVED ADVANTAGES OF JUNIOR COLLEGES The popularity of junior colleges among state politicians, it appeared, was largely the result of their great variety of functions. Conservatives and liberals generally agreed upon their importance, although the basis of their approval often varied considerably.

The heterogeneity of this approval became even more apparent when the respondents' reasons for supporting junior colleges were examined directly. The state leaders gave a variety of different answers, the most common being economy, educational opportunity, easing the transition of students from high school to college, and assisting the "latebloomer."

Economy The most commonly mentioned advantage of the junior college was its economy. Indeed the perception of the junior colleges as economical appeared to be one of the main reasons that many budget-conscious legislators spoke so favorably of them. Although responses on this question ranged from a Kansas legislator's emphatic "very much so," to a Pennsylvania state Senator's observation that "there's nothing economical about anything in education," most of the leaders agreed that the junior colleges were more economical for both the state and the student. Those who emphasized the economy of junior colleges to the state pointed out that they saved expenses connected with such facilities as residence halls and student unions; those who emphasized the economy of the junior colleges to the student pointed out that they saved traveling and living expenses for the local resident.

A few legislators differed, saying that junior colleges were more economical for the student but questioning whether in fact they saved the state any money. "I am quite sure that it costs less to educate at the University of Kansas," argued one respondent, "than it does in a junior college." Others similarly thought that the state could educate students just as cheaply during the first two years in four-year institutions.

Educational Opportunity

The respondents noted, favorably and almost unanimously, that whether the junior colleges were economical to the state or not, they made post-high school education available to a greater number of people. This was viewed by many as even more important than economy. More than one respondent said that college education was becoming a necessity, not a luxury, and that consequently the states had an obligation to increase the availability of higher education. The junior colleges were regarded as a principal way of meeting this responsibility. A New York Senator declared: "Education for all, that's the virtue [of the junior colleges]. . . . Let each person become what he is capable of being" (a paraphrase of the motto of the State University of New York). Asked about other advantages of the junior colleges, the Senator continued:

My main point [about] the community college is not even economics. Maybe [the junior college system] isn't economical, I don't know. . . . I like it when a kid gets out of high school, he has an opportunity to go on to school in a community college.

A California legislator echoed this viewpoint: "They at least give everyone an opportunity for the first leg up." A Kentucky Senator saw this advantage: "People who cannot afford to leave home and go to a metropolitan center to attend a major university can get, now, the first two years. . . . Living at home eliminates a major portion of the expense of an education." Another Kentucky official took much the same position on availability of education to low-income students provided by junior colleges:

They permit a greater number of children who are not financially able to leave their homes and live at a regional university to at least try college, to determine whether or not they're capable of doing college work and capable of going ahead. I think children who do well in community colleges probably can obtain financial aid to finish their college training, where these same children who had not been tested and tried at the community college level might never make it to college.

Easing the Transition from High School to College

A third major advantage of the junior colleges, according to many respondents, was that they provided an educational opportunity for those students who might have difficulty making the transition from high school to a large university or college. Such students could take the first two years at a school near their homes and then transfer to a four-year institution. A Kentucky Republican, himself a product of a junior college, explained why such a transitional period might be necessary: "Some students are not ready, not prepared, for the large college, with masses of students. The community college provides a transition; after a couple of years, they may be ready for a large college or university." A California Assemblyman elaborated on this theme:

It's easier for the student to make the adjustment from high school into junior college because he hasn't severed all his family and community relationships, and he can make a more gradual adjustment to being on his own than if you take him completely out of his home community and dump him as a stranger into some other town.

Similar comments were made by a number of officials who observed that the junior colleges provided an opportunity for young persons undecided about their education or occupational goals to "get a start" and to determine what they really wanted to do.

Assisting the "Latebloomer" The opportunity provided for the "latebloomer" and for "the person who didn't make it in high school" also was cited by several respondents as among the chief advantages of junior colleges. A California legislator called the junior colleges a "salvaging ground" where people could catch up and perhaps move into the University:

I am one of these people myself. It was this open-door policy where people come in—they want to straighten up, fly right, do remedial work, move off—they can. It's not a high school with ash trays, as some people describe it; it has a definite mission, and if a student can't make it there, why then he doesn't want to go anywhere with any direction, I feel. It's a recovery ground, salvage area—the ones who do go on do very well in the University level and the state college level.

A Pennsylvania Senator similarly thought that the junior colleges were "a darned good idea" because they gave the "latebloomer" a second chance to prove himself.

THE COORDINATION OF THE JUNIOR COLLEGES Whether or not they endorsed expanding the junior colleges in numbers and scope, the legislators and executives with whom we talked were almost unanimous in stressing the need for state-level planning and coordination of the numerical growth, geographic distribution, curricula, academic standards, and financing. They agreed that the junior colleges must somehow be integrated into an overall state system of higher education. The amount of coordination varied considerably from state to state. California, Illinois, Iowa, Kentucky, Louisiana, New York, and Texas all had central coordinating boards with varying degrees of governing authority over the junior colleges. Two states—Kansas and Pennsylvania—had no central planning or coordinating bodies. In all nine states, the junior colleges were primarily, if not exclusively, financed by the communities in which they were located and by student fees.

Political Pressures There was much concern that without state-level planning and control, each state would end up with more junior colleges than it needed or could afford and that their geographical distribution would be determined by political rather than educational factors. As one Kentucky administrator admitted, "There has probably been a little too much politics in deciding the sites [of junior colleges]." An Iowa legislator was more strongly critical of this trend. "It's asinine that they would locate [one] in a community of 900."

Several legislators noted that political pressures tended to promote growth of the junior colleges. "These area vocational schools are something that were greeted with more enthusiasm than any other suggestions I had ever seen by the people of Iowa. They want them. They like schools close to them."

According to some of our respondents, state-level coordination was needed not only to control numerical expansion, but also to control the tendency of the two-year schools to "mushroom" into four-year colleges. Local communities not only want junior colleges, explained another Iowan, they want their junior college "to grow and prosper" and ideally to become a full-fledged four-year college or maybe even a university with graduate programs. Most leaders felt that their states simply could not afford to let too many four-year institutions develop.

In Kentucky, where there was pressure to convert some of the junior colleges into four-year colleges, one of our respondents was asked if the state could afford to do this. He replied: "I'll have to say no, definitely. I am definitely not in favor of setting up more four-year colleges or expanding community colleges into four-year colleges." An Iowa legislator also expressed opposition to expanding junior colleges into four-year schools.

Louisiana leaders were particulary apprehensive that any new junior colleges might develop into four-year schools. (This was the case with six of the state junior colleges established in Louisiana since 1900.) One Louisiana Democrat, asked if he was in favor of more junior colleges, declared:

Well, I have been. I understand they work well in other states, but they haven't worked well here because a junior college, because of the lack of coordination that we have, immediately becomes a senior college, and then they immediately get into the graduate field, and the next thing you know, that junior college that you established, that there was a need for in that area, for a junior college, but not beyond that—and next thing you know they're granting doctorates.

Although they thought that some new junior colleges might be needed, this apprehension, plus the feeling that building new schools would be too expensive, seemed the main reasons why many Louisiana leaders responded hesitantly to the idea of expanding junior colleges.

An Iowa legislator criticized what he saw as a similar tendency in his own state. He felt that the development of junior colleges had not been adequately controlled:

They're all going to end up with football teams and all the other stuff that goes with it. And it's a chamber of commerce type thing that towns have got the school; they want them to grow and prosper, just like the towns that have the higher education institutions. It's a business to them.

Academic Standards State-level regulation of the curricula and academic standards of the junior colleges was also among needs cited by several legislators who wanted more "coordination." It was suggested—especially by those who cast the junior colleges in academic, college-transfer roles—that control of curricula and quality was essential to the transfer function. A Texan explained the need for coordination in some detail:

I think here that the coordinating board has not gone as far as it should. A student graduating from a junior college has no possibility of knowing which credits will be accepted at what college within the state system, much less private schools. You can go to one school and 52 hours will be accepted, and at another, 43 hours will be accepted, and the hours accepted at one will not be accepted at another. I think that this is a great waste of facilities, resources, and manpower.

A New York administrator also stressed the importance of standardizing junior college offerings and coordinating them with the programs of senior colleges. He was optimistic about achieving such coordination and control in New York.

The general feeling among respondents was, as a California legislator put it, "for moving the junior colleges . . . into a position of becoming full-fledged partners in higher education." Most of them felt this could best be achieved through some kind of statewide coordinating board or board of regents. There were some, however, who saw the way to achieve coordination as giving senior institutions governing authority over the junior colleges. Such a position was taken by a Pennsylvania legislator who felt the junior colleges would be more efficient than "feeder colleges."

Support for state-level coordination was in many cases coupled with advocacy of increased state appropriations to the two-year schools. This was interesting in view of the fact that one of the principal virtues mentioned by advocates of the junior college was economy to the state—an economy due in great part to the fact that existing junior colleges were financed largely by local property taxes and student fees. In Texas, where approximately one-third of junior college expenses were financed by the state, the leaders we interviewed favored a massive increase in state money to them. A state Senator who expected junior colleges to take care of increasing college enrollments declared:

I am in favor of upgrading the financial support of junior colleges from the state. Cities, as you know, are swamped by the demands for spending in the public schools. They will not be able to handle the problem of financing a junior college, and I think that it is therefore the state's obligation to help in the financial support of junior colleges.

A member of the Iowa legislature expressed a fairly typical view on financing junior colleges with state money:

Well, the degree of growth they experience during any given period is of course directly related to the amount of money they have available. There we find the same problem of course with any of the state universities, any of the state schools. I suspect that the growth of the area schools will be hindered somewhat by a lack of financial reserves. There will be an attempt,

I'm sure, to adequately fund them, but I'm sure we'll never meet their immediate needs 100 percent.

The majority of state officials thus favored some kind of effort to coordinate the activities of junior colleges with those of other institutions of higher education in their respective states. The major cause of the disarray, according to many respondents, was the tendency for local communities to seek a junior college of their own or to petition the legislature to transform the local college into a four-year institution.

CONCLUSION It was apparent that the junior colleges presented a major challenge to legislative foresight and ingenuity. Interviews showed strong support by most segments of the legislature and by the general public. Junior colleges were variously credited with being economical, with providing educational opportunities to lower-income students, with assisting those who have not done well in high school or who find the transition to college difficult, and with training nonacademically oriented students in vocational skills. Obviously junior colleges had a positive appeal to legislators of all political persuasions. From the perspective of the local community, furthermore, they were seen as extremely valuable assets — both to local industry and business and to civic pride. Thus communities competed over the location of junior colleges and, at times, over their expansion into four-year institutions. Such political pressures were difficult for legislators to ignore.

The obvious dilemma facing junior colleges, as a result — one well recognized by the politicians themselves — was that these schools were frequently allowed to develop without any definition as to their educational goals and any sustained planning as to location and integration into the states' educational systems. If junior colleges are to be fully and efficiently utilized, such definition, planning, and coordination seem essential. To limit the role of junior colleges, or to predetermine their locations would probably serve to erode some of the widespread popularity and support which they now receive. Thus difficult political decisions must be made before these problems can be overcome.

In general, legislators recognize that the popularity of junior colleges lies in their appeal to various political, business, and civic groups. To eliminate some of these appeals may make the junior colleges more efficient, more academic, or more rational in terms of the states' educational goals, but it may also reduce the widespread political support they now receive. Future planning, including coordination, thus seems in order (and inevitable), but it will have to be well conceived, well timed, and well executed if it is to succeed.

8. Student Unrest: Causes and Cures

Student misconduct, as noted earlier, is among the few topics on which citizens communicate with state representatives in the area of higher education. Among the state officials themselves, furthermore, the issue of student activism elicited the longest and most emotional responses in the entire survey. As one legislator aptly put it, "Everybody's an expert on unrest." Almost every legislative and executive official interviewed had an opinion about the causes of student unrest, what to do about it, and what its effects upon the legislature were likely to be. While other areas of the survey often suffered from lack of clear perceptions or beliefs, state politicians responded to these questions at length and often with great intensity.

The majority clearly desired the enforcement of more discipline by university officials, including the dismissal of those who violated school regulations or engaged in unlawful acts. The majority also thought that the demonstrations had a negative effect upon the legislators within their respective states. Although those who favored legislative action against the activists were reported to be in a minority in all nine states at the time of the survey, many warned that increased unrest would likely result in some kind of legislative involvement. Since then, these prophecies have been fulfilled in many states. In this chapter we will review the major reasons the respondents gave for the causes of student unrest and their views of how to remedy the problem insofar as it affects the university and the legislature.

CAUSES OF STUDENT UNREST The respondents gave a variety of often conflicting interpretations of the student disruptions. Some thought that the demonstrations were a result of the hypocrisies of middle-class society; others saw them as a part of the general decline in morality within

127

the country. Some dismissed the protests as symptoms of youthful rebellion; others praised the student activists for their concern with public affairs. Some faulted the universities for being too permissive, others for not providing instruction relevant to the students' needs and for not being themselves involved in the issues of the day.

The Hypocrisies of American Society A small but highly articulate group of legislators blamed the student disorders on the failure of American society to live up to its own professed ideals. To them the student protest movement was "an objective look at some of the hypocrisy of our society." These officials not only sympathized with the student rebels but shared their outrage at the course of events. They were especially critical of the overemphasis on material goods in America and saw the students as one of the few groups to reject such materialism and to seek something better of life. The most articulate spokesman for this position was a Senator from New York:

What has happened suddenly in the past four or five years is that we have begun to crack at the seams . . . we have a very great commitment to middle-class life—which is the house, the car, and the kids going to a nice school and on to college and getting married to a nice boy who has a nice job, who can buy the house, etc. We ignore [the fact] that there is one-third of our society who cannot achieve [this] even though [it] is our philosophical commitment. . . .

The kids on campus, I think, are beginning to realize that maybe this great life that has been promised to them by their parents of the house in the suburb with the trimmed lawn is not . . . all that they want. I think it is a spiritual malaise, really; I think that is what it comes to . . . the kids are beginning to want some faith—they want something to believe in. . . .

The adult world at this time doesn't quite understand what is happening and refuses to—let me say it is almost like the response to the problem of the ghetto.

The reason that the students were able to see these contradictions, according to this legislator, was because they hadn't yet developed a stake in society. Rather they were still asking themselves what they wanted to be doing in 30 or 40 years. This theme was further developed by a Texas legislator:

Basically the students are caught in a trap, a theoretical trap that they can't describe but can feel. . . . Our academic tradition is that we are trying to turn out enlightened people . . . people who can think for themselves and develop their minds. What kind of society do we dump then into? . . . They know that IBM doesn't really want the educated mind; it wants the trained mind. And they know that if you go to work for Proctor & Gamble, you are not going to have the chance for many years to express the kind of freedom that [they] have been told to respect.

I ask you to take a look at a society which is regimented, where the individual intellectual freedom of a citizen is almost nonexistent. They look at newspapers which don't tell what they think are the facts. They look at the churches which deny their very purpose for existence. They look at adults who are more interested in liquor by the drink and horse racing than they are about the underprivileged members of society. And they rebel.

A Senator from California took much the same position:

I think that the students of today are just too smart to see themselves pigeonholed into the programming of the past. If we are truly a Judeo-Christian nation, we should live by the concepts of those faiths. If we are truly a democracy, we should live by the conceptions of that political philosophy. And they are smart enough to see that we are not doing either one.

The problem, this legislator thought, was one of a generation gap. And too many men in the Senate, he added, were over 45.

Two minority group legislators were among this group of student supporters. Both strongly attacked the hypocrisies of American society in emphasizing such values as equality and freedom while practicing something quite different.

The Moral Decline   In stark contrast to the supporters of student dissent were those strongly opposed to the demonstrations. While the previous group of legislators blamed the unrest upon the failure of society to live up to its ideals, these respondents blamed it upon the failure of society to transmit its values to the younger generation.

The former group criticized the schools, the church, and the government for not providing moral leadership, but these officials criticized them for not teaching the young to respect their country and the advantages they had been given. Thus while the first group of legislators saw the students as the moral conscience of contemporary society, the second group saw them as representative of the moral decline of contemporary society. The response of a Texas Assemblyman illustrates this second concern:

A lot of them haven't had anything to do all their lives except go to school, or party, or whatever they wanted to do. . . . They have no responsibility at home, and so why should they have responsibility after they go to college? . . . Somewhere down the line, we have failed to . . . teach them to respect our country and to respect the advantages that they have been given—to respect those things they have been handed on a silver platter. . . . I think it goes back to perhaps the home, perhaps the public school, perhaps the church, but most especially . . . the home itself.

Similarly, a Pennsylvania Senator declared:

The adults and people away from these communities feel very, very strongly that these students are not qualified to pass judgment on these things—that they are not attacking a decadent society. What they're actually doing is that they're trying to substitute their opinions and their judgment as to what is best against the results of years and years and years of trial and error and experience. And instead of being free, independent thinkers, they are being pretty irresponsible.

According to a number of these critics, a major reason for unrest was that students had had life too easy and thus failed to appreciate what they have been given. This theme emerged from the following:

Interviewer: How would you account for this unrest?

Respondent: Too much and too many material things that they have had all of their lives, and they don't have the desire for an education. That is the only thing that I can attribute it to. I went to school out here and everybody was too busy working, trying to get through, to have a great deal of unrest.

Interviewer: Why would it be different now?

Respondent: Because we are living in a more affluent society. Kids have been given too many automobiles and too much money to spend and too much leisure time. . . . I don't know what it is in other countries, but I think that we are all living too soft and having it too easy for the past 25 years.

A result of this greater freedom, leisure, and affluence among the younger generation, a number of officials asserted, was a widespread lack of respect for authority. A Pennsylvania Assemblyman said:

I know that when I was a child in school my relationship with the teachers was almost that of the relationship with my parents. I would no more think of being disrespectful to my instructor or teacher than I would of being disrespectful to my parents. With children today that is not the order of the day. They are just as disrespectful to parents and to teachers as you can imagine a child being. Disrespectful of the man in a uniform. The law does not impose the kind of authority that it should to these children.

An Illinois legislator said life would be a lot easier if the students were to show more respect for authority and conventions.

A few respondents associated the student disorders with their own conservative political philosophies. It was the activities of politicians and civil rights advocates, they asserted, that created the atmosphere for the demonstrations. An Iowa Republican, for example, thought that a lot of the restlessness was caused by the policies of the existing administration and the philosophy of government which had predominated for the past 30 years. He blamed the student disorders on the new economics, deficit financing, and the Supreme Court.

Two other officials felt that the civil rights movement was largely responsible for the disorders. An Illinois Republican said that the "ignoring of laws" by those involved in the movement had served as a bad example to the youth—who were naturally "belligerent about certain things . . . at a certain stage of their life."

A Louisiana official thought that the whole problem was created by politicians who promised "too much too fast" to the Negroes to win their votes. The psychology of lack of respect for authority and law, he asserted, had filtered down to the kids and influenced their activities.

The Vietnam War

One of the more obvious explanations for student unrest was the war in Vietnam. As one Kansas legislator put it, "This is the first time in our history that we have a war going on that the majority of our people have their doubts about." Since students were being called upon to fight in such a "dubious" war, it seemed natural that they would be among the first to object to it. And since the universities themselves had served as the principal centers of dissent, the students could not help but be exposed to antiwar arguments.

Despite these compelling factors—and despite the fact that virtually all of the incidents discussed by the respondents were connected with antiwar protests—only a few legislators gave prominent attention to the war as a major cause of student dissatisfaction. Most simply mentioned the war in passing or associated the war's effect with the general "trend of the times" (to be considered below). The existence of the war in Vietnam might have become so much a part of these respondents' perception of reality that they no longer took into account its unique impact on American society—including its unsettling effect on those who must decide whether or not to serve in the armed forces. On the other hand, the legislators might have simply refrained from discussing what they considered "politics" with their academic (and possibly hostile) interviewer.

At any rate, the legislators spent more time discussing other causes of student unrest than they did the war in Vietnam. And those who mentioned the war generally refrained from bringing their own opinions into the discussion. Most of these respondents placed major emphasis upon the uncertainties that the war created in the student's career. Such a position was taken by a Kansas Assemblyman:

Some of it is just uncertainty and not knowing what the future holds. There is a war going on, and they don't know if they will be allowed to complete their education.

An Illinois Senator:

The fact that a war is staring him in the face is the big cause of it. A young man goes after some higher education, works hard, saves his money, maybe works some; the only thing he can look forward to is a war—getting killed, getting shot.

And a Texas Senator:

There has always been a lot of unrest, particularly in wartime. You have a very unsettling problem of a boy knowing that he can make no plans.

A Kansas Senator did not think that the students were mature enough to handle the pressures they experienced. An Iowa Assemblyman thought that the inability of anyone to explain the war was a major cause of discontent. And a California Senator believed that the students resented the fact that they might be "atomized overnight."

Undoubtedly, other legislators would have given similar responses if they had been probed specifically upon the effects of the war. Many did mention the war in passing or in other contexts.

A Trend of the Times

A slightly larger number of respondents gave a more general explanation: that the student protests were associated with the general feeling of unrest characteristic of the period. Unrest existed everywhere, according to these legislators, and the college campuses simply shared in this general feeling of uneasiness. For most this unrest was vaguely related to tensions throughout the world. Representative of this view was the response of a Pennsylvania Assemblyman:

I think you'll find there is student unrest, there's no doubt about that. But you'll find that there's unrest in this country, not just among students. Look at the number of demonstrations that we have which are not on college campuses. After all, these things are connected. It's difficult to say just why we have so much unrest, but you will find with our racial strife, with the Vietnam war, with the tensions in the world, the uncertainties of what's going to happen in the future—this tends to cause unrest and then when you have people who are restless, this is contagious.

A Kansas Assemblyman thought that such problems would especially affect the inquisitive mind of the student:

We are living in a time where a lot of questions are going unanswered. There are problems abroad and at home—in our cities. There is unrest and so forth. You take the young person we are speaking of, he wants an education, yet he reads the newspapers and hears the news and he is concerned. He has an inquisitive mind, and when he can't get adequate answers, he has got to show that he is concerned.

A second Kansan asserted that the current unrest resulted from a loss of faith in democracy. The remainder of this group offered no specific reasons for the unrest but simply saw the demonstrations as a tendency of the times—a "demonstration tendency" as a Pennsylvania Assemblyman called it.

The Nature of Youth

A sizable number of legislators considered the demonstrations to be little more than symptoms of youthful rebellion and irresponsibility. "The nature of youth is unrest," said an Iowa official. "I think it is a natural condition of youth," agreed a Kansas colleague. An

Illinois legislator compared the student demonstrators to the goldfish swallowers of his day:

Well, I suppose because for one reason they're kids. I don't know why my peers ate goldfish when I was in school either. I really don't . . . but I've seen them do it, you know. . . . But young people have a lot of vitality, you know, and a lot of energy to get rid of, and this is one way they have of doing it. I don't know the reason.

None of these respondents was particularly disturbed by the disruptions. One legislator said, "Personally, I don't think students are any different now than they ever were. I think we ought to give them the right to let off their steam so that they can keep their sanity." Another believed that the altercations were largely "unrest for unrest's sake" and would eventually settle down. A third said that student unrest had existed throughout history and posed no great threat to society, but could perhaps be channeled in a "more constructive" direction.

While a few of these legislators pointed to the utility of youthful unrest, the majority of this group dismissed the demonstrations in much the same way that an earlier generation dismissed those who ate goldfish. A Pennsylvania official proclaimed that he was probably as great a "hell-raiser" in his day—but that the things to raise hell about had changed.

The Generation Gap A major response pattern was found among those who associated student unrest with what is often termed the "generation gap." These responses were more heterogeneous than those discussed above. They were predominantly sympathetic, but cautious, attempts to explain the student disorders in terms of the different perceptions and experiences of youth. Some officials welcomed the new mode of thought among young people and asserted that students today were more aware of public affairs than they previously had been. Others accepted the students' right to dissent but were troubled by their more extreme forms of behavior.

Prominent among the first group were assemblymen from Texas, Iowa, and New York. The Texan said:

Part of it stems from what I would characterize as the older generation's lack of understanding. And I think that there is just a new tendency to search and inquire that you haven't had before. Personally, I think that it is healthy. I fall in with the students just on an emotional basis more than with the other side. . . . There is a certain intolerance on the part of the older generation to want to teach and talk and not to listen, and the younger generation not only in my judgment wants to talk but they should be listened to.

The Iowan believed that the extreme efforts of the young to become nonconformists were a result of their "more objective look at what life really is." The New York legislator asserted that most of the students were "good kids wanting to learn" and that the older generation should try to understand the new world that they live in and must cope with.

Other officials were less inclined to praise youth but similarly welcomed young people's greater interest and involvement in public affairs. An Assemblyman from New York said, "the average young-ster today is more aware of what's going on and is more exposed to what's going on" than he was. A Kentucky Senator gave a similar response to the interviewer: "I think that the youth of our day is maybe thinking a little more than folks thought back when I was going to school and when you were going to school." And an Iowa Assemblyman thought that the greater education of today's youth had something to do with their willingness to assert themselves:

There isn't as much respect for the opinions of the elders, so they want to assert themselves. And the reason might be that we're educating them probably better at as young an age. I think the average 18-year-old has more education today than we had in our time, and maybe they do feel actually superior and think they see some faults in the way government is run and all.

A Texas Assemblyman thought that each generation spoke a dif-ferent language than the preceding one. Such change, he believed, was good. A California Assemblyman said that the activists he knew were "extremely bright" and that the greater affluence and intellectual ability among today's students left them with more time to become involved.

A second group of legislators praised the greater awareness of contemporary youth but felt uneasy about the uncompromising nature of their demands and wished they wouldn't go quite so far as they did. This ambivalence is reflected in the following exchange with a New York Senator:

Interviewer: There is a lot of unrest on the campuses today and it seems to be nationwide. How do you account for it? What's the cause of it? What do you see as the causal agent here?

Respondent: Well, I guess it's breaking away from the establishment. The emphasis that we are all placing on an individual's freedom of action or reaction. I think we stress this—that you can be what you want to be, do what you want to do. That's what this country is all about, and for a long while they did it in the context of the established order. Many still are—most still are—but some have spun off.

Interviewer: Which aspects of that order are the ones you see?

Respondent: Well, even our customs. I'm not talking about our establishment in the sense of the customs of morals and behavior and how you're going to treat your body, how you're going to look; I mean these people, the individuals today, are letting this individual thing carry them into what people of my generation would call extremes. It doesn't bother me, except as I sense the fact that we can't afford yet in this world for all of us to be this way as long as there are forces abroad . . . that could, if given their sway, destroy what we've got here and what we're trying to have here, and that is what bothers me about it.

Interviewer: What do you think ought to be done about it?

Respondent: I think you've got to have teachers in our schools and in our colleges who are persuasive enough and bright enough and sophisticated enough to sense this and yet to point out that there are even greater values that they may have to temporize a bit with these new freedoms to preserve. . . . I think this is too much for a kid fresh out of high school to understand, but it isn't too much for a professor to understand. . . . Let's not lose sight of some of these more basic things that we have to think about in this kind of world.

Other officials welcomed the students' concern but expressed similar reservations. An Iowa Senator—whose own children were among the demonstrators—said:

I certainly think that people my age are having a time adjusting to this and are rather shocked when a lot of things that we thought of tremendous value are scorned by younger people. Shocked and disturbed and bothered by it. And no matter how broadminded you try to be, it's still there. There's certainly a lot of nervousness about it.

College students, he felt, had always been radical. But among today's students "there is more genuine turning away from things their parents thought were valuable."

Most of these officials either gave no reason for the so-called generation gap or saw it largely in terms of the greater education and awareness of contemporary youth and the greater problems with which he must cope. A few respondents, however, thought these differences resulted from failure to solve the nation's problems and from the relative lack of economic motivation among youth. Three legislators offered the first explanation. An Illinois Assemblyman felt that the unrest arose largely out of America's failure to get along with other countries and other races and out of a desire among the young to do better themselves. An Iowa Senator gave a similar explanation:

I think . . . these kids are disillusioned—disappointed in their elders, in the way that some of us older ones have been running the country—and it's just natural they're going to raise questions and raise hell in some cases.

And a colleague in the Iowa Senate asserted:

The old are the majority and the electorate and say, "children." . . . With the military involvement and with the draft, it's uncertain that they will ever come back. It kind of makes you look at our state's and our nation's effort, and I understand them. And as a result, because they are affected by the decisions made by the so-called mature, over-21, legal-voting-age citizens, they can rebel and I don't object to this at all as long as they . . . don't violate the law and things like this.

A few legislators believed that the generation gap emerged from the differences in economic motivations between those raised in the Depression and those raised in today's affluent society. The main proponent of this argument was a California Assemblyman who pointed out that his generation's "flower children" all died (in spirit) in the bread lines of the 1930s:

This generation doesn't understand those of us who were reared in the Depression. The principal motivation is economic and our concern for grabbing everything we can as quickly as possible and hanging on to it as desperately as we do. We are afraid it's all going to evaporate and go back to the bread lines again. They don't see the fact that our flower children all died in the bread lines in the 1930s.

A Pennsylvania legislator differentiated his student days on precisely this economic ground: "Of course, I was one of those people who went to school to get an education so I could make a couple of bucks." But a New York Senator said what he liked about today's youth was that they "think about things other than making a living."

Other Factors All the above causes of student unrest were mentioned by enough respondents to be considered in detail. Four other factors, however, were brought up by a smaller number of officials: the role of the media, the demonstrators' desire for publicity, troublemakers and agitators, and faculty encouragement.

A number of legislators noted that people were more aware of public issues today than they had ever been before. Two went further, claiming the media played an important role in stimulating protests. A Pennsylvania Assemblyman also held that the media made young people more aware of disaster:

I'm inclined to think that perhaps the world of television has had a lot to do with it. The world of communication has had a lot to do with this because perhaps these young people — now living in a world of violence with threatened extermination by atomic weapons and hydrogen bombs — have, through the communication media and television, a more ready awareness of what this disaster may be.

A Texas official thought the media important in fermenting unrest by making everyone aware of what was going on. "The Vietnam conflict," he pointed out, "is being fought in the living room of every home in the country."

Three other respondents had a quite different interpretation of the role of the media in creating unrest. These officials thought that a major motivation of the demonstrators was to gain publicity. An Iowa Senator felt that some students and professors participated largely to get their names into the papers:

I think that there's a minority of these students and there's a minority of these professors that would like to get some publicity. And if they get their name in the paper once, why then they want to do it again and see if they can get it in there again.

An Illinois Senator — who was extremely critical of the student and faculty demonstrations — was even more adamant in this respect. "If we didn't have TV cameras all over the place," he asserted, "we wouldn't have half the problems we've got." And a California Senator thought that students had always wished to leave their "mark" but that the media now allowed them to do this "on a much more dramatic basis."

A few officials thought that the unrest resulted largely from the actions of a few troublemakers and agitators. A Pennsylvania Assemblyman thought the demonstrations occurred because "there are too many troublemakers in the universities today." An Illinois legislator believed the protests were encouraged by a few people "who haven't shown good judgment." The protesters, he asserted, had an establishment "just as great as any establishment they were attacking. They have their gospel; they have their bible; they have their idols . . . they are nowhere different from adult society in some respects."

Four respondents placed the primary blame for the demonstrations upon the faculty. The most vocal was a California Assemblyman:

I blame the faculty and the administration. . . . They are only passing the buck between themselves. The administration says that they can't act because they would destroy faculty morale and academic freedom. They're afraid of the faculty. Or else it's just a way of passing the buck. And the faculty aren't going to do anything—they're only encouraging it. . . .

Yes, I think the faculty are directly responsible for the unrest. We have actual evidence of the faculty egging the students on. . . . You know that none of the faculty were fired for their actions on the Berkeley campus, none at all?

An Illinois Assemblyman said: "You have a lunatic fringe on the campus. On the faculty, I mean. These people don't have any sense of proprieties. The faculty is more at fault than the students. Definitely." Both officials were extremely critical of the demonstrations in their states. Two Louisiana legislators also thought faculty responsible for the unrest but did not elaborate on their charges.

THE CURES State legislators thus disagreed strongly among themselves over the causes of student unrest. How, then, did they think the demonstrations should be remedied? Did they feel the universities had been too permissive in their handling of student unrest? Did they expect the legislature to become involved in this issue? What did they feel would be the effect of student activism upon legislation affecting higher education in general?

It would be surprising, of course, if university administrations were not criticized for their part in the student troubles. The majority of legislative leaders clearly thought that the universities had been too permissive with the student rebels and, it would appear, favored the dismissal of those who broke university regulations. One group forcefully demanded the outright expulsion of all those involved in demonstrations. A second group was less vocal and emotional in its responses but similarly called for greater discipline and, when necessary, dismissal. A third group was more sympathetic. These officials defended the students' right to demonstrate peacefully but would have stronger measures taken against those who broke the law or violated the rights of others. A final group of legislators thought that the universities could best respond to the unrest by being more responsive to the students and themselves becoming more involved in public issues.

About one-third of those interviewed were asked whether they thought the students should be given more of a say in university policies. The overwhelming response of this group was that they should not. A few officials would allow them an "advisory" role but only one respondent would give students a voice in decisions concerning instructors and courses.

**The Demand
for More
Discipline**
About a tenth of the respondents had a clear and simple solution for the demonstrations: expel those who made trouble. If the students wanted to go to college, they argued, they should obey the rules. If they refused, they should be expelled; the taxpayers should not be made to support such misconduct.

A Texas legislator was among the more vociferous exponents of this viewpoint:

If the student just goes on a rampage, then if he starts destroying property and actually cursing his government, I think he ought to be expelled. . . . I don't think any state should have to appropriate money to furnish a kid an audience or to furnish him a place to demonstrate. . . . I think that they should be expelled; I think that they should be handled by the law. . . . I don't believe in coddling them at all. I don't think that you are going to see too much of that here in Texas either.

An Illinois Assemblyman was among the more emotional respondents on the issue:

Everybody's an expert on unrest. Every day somebody gets up and tells us what's poor about the country. There's a peace march; there's draft cards;

there's a U.S. marshal. Hell! Students are demonstrating against Dow Chemical. I'd kick their behinds out of school. I'd fire the professors too. Academic freedom is just used as an excuse for flouting the law.

A slightly larger group of respondents expressed similar views but were not as extreme in their demands. These officials called for greater discipline by the university authorities — including (at times) the dismissal of those who went too far — but were not as upset by the demonstrations as the previous group. Typically, these legislators replied that the students shouldn't be allowed to run the university.

"I feel that you've got to have respect for authority if you expect something to function," asserted a Louisianian. "I don't think you can turn something over to a mob regardless of what the mob may be," said a colleague. A third Louisianian thought that it might be better if college authorities brought in speakers "more interested in constitutional government and the betterment of the country" than those "bent on tearing it down."

A New York Assemblyman likewise believed that there should be more discipline: "There is no question that if you want to go to school, you just have to accept the rules — otherwise get out, you don't belong there." He didn't think the demonstrations were a big problem in New York, however, since they (then) involved such a small number of students.

Other legislators were concerned about the fact that university officials sometimes submitted to the demands of the protesters. A California Senator faulted the University officials for condoning the demonstrations on grounds that they were "expressions of the university or college way of life." This type of reasoning, he thought, was specious — particularly when it involved acquiescing to the demands of the activists. An Iowa Senator similarly asserted: "The administration of the various schools has got to make it clear that the kids can't take the law into their own hands and can't run the institution. This would be the worst thing that could happen."

The Demand for Punishing Lawbreakers

A third group of respondents was more sympathetic to the students but was concerned about the violence and lawlessness of some of their protests. These officials defended the students' right to demonstrate peacefully but would have stronger measures taken against those who broke the law or violated the rights of others. The best statement of this position came from a Kansas Assemblyman:

I think the right of peaceful protest and demonstration is inherent in our system. It has to be retained. On the other hand, there is a corollary right of the protection of person and property that has to be maintained. If that protest or demonstration takes the form of infringing on the rights or protection of person and property, yes, then I think the police should come in.

A California Assemblyman said that the demonstrators had "no right to disrupt the pattern of the whole educational institution" and that he would protect the right of others who wanted to attend the University. A New York Assemblyman didn't think that suppressing the demonstrations would accomplish anything, but resented the "riots," "sit-ins," and "disorderliness."

An Iowa legislator said he was disturbed by the principle of civil disobedience frequently used to justify the sit-ins and take-overs of university buildings: "I don't think that when you say there are certain laws you don't have to obey, that this will ever get us anything but destruction because who's to judge what laws are to be obeyed and what laws aren't?"

The Demand for Greater Relevance One group of respondents emphasized the need for universities to be more responsive to the students and to become more involved in public issues themselves. This was the smallest of the patterns of response, and many of these officials noted that their opinion was a minority viewpoint within their own states. The principal exponent of this position was the New York Senator quoted previously on the hypocrisies of American society. The major problem, he thought, was that the faculty had not recognized its responsibility as adults. Students were looking for some guidance or control, but their elders were using permissiveness as an excuse for noninvolvement. The problem today, he believed, was that most of the prohibitions set up by adults were irrational: "The adult world no longer knows what is a rational limit and what is not."

Other officials indicated that what was taught in the universities was not always relevant to the students' needs. A California Assemblyman said:

And far too often professors lecture with the same notes that they've used forever, and the relating of what is being taught to current problems isn't there. And the damn thing is just a total vacuum and out of context and [the student is] bound to have a reaction to this.

A New York Assemblyman made much the same argument. The universities, he asserted, were isolated despite their attempts to become involved in public service. "They have a terrible cultural lag—one of the worst there is." An Illinois legislator thought that one of the factors behind the "student power" movement was the failure of the universities to introduce new ideas. The students, he felt, were smart enough to see this and had many ideas of their own:

[The students ask,] "Why should we go to class to waste our time when we can be doing it better?" Many of them have ideas. . . . These kids aren't dummies out there. They're smarter than a lot of you Ph.D.'s in some areas —but they know you're not doing the job, and I have to agree with them.

An Iowa Assemblyman, finally, believed that the answer might be a strong administration which became more involved with the students: "I think there has to be more identification with students. This is probably why they have missed the boat."

Student Participation in Policy Decisions

About one-third of the respondents were asked whether they felt that students should be given a greater voice in setting university policies. The overwhelming response of this group was that they should not be.

Most officials simply dismissed the question with an unequivocal "No." Some added that the students were not mature enough to assume such responsibilities. "If you let the students decide," said a New York Senator, "unless they are more mature than I think, they're bound to set up a set of standards that would destroy what should be done in an institution of higher education." A Kansas Senator thought that it was nice to "make them think they are participating" but would leave control with "well-paid professional administrators."

Others would grant the students very limited responsibilities in running their own affairs. A Texas legislator, for example, would allow the students to publish the *Daily Texan*—the censorship of which had been an issue in the state—"as long as they are reasonable and don't advocate overthrow and don't advocate some of this radical stuff we hear."

A commonly expressed viewpoint was that the students should be given an "advisory role" but should not be allowed to decide actual policy. Thus a Kansan thought students should be consulted when they were directly affected by policy but "should never be allowed to go further and dictate the policy." A colleague said, "I think that students generally are pretty responsible people and at least in their junior and senior years would be in a position to make valuable recommendations concerning the operations of the schools." Only one legislator, however—a first-term Assemblyman from Texas—favored giving students a voice in policy decisions:

If you have some constructive ways to channel this unrest, it wouldn't be so much of a problem. . . . The students ought to control their own news-paper without any intervention from Frank Irwin [chairman of the board of trustees]. And they ought to have some voice in making decisions about instructors, about courses, and the like.

THE LEGISLATURE AND STUDENT UNREST

Probably the most important questions concerned the likelihood of legislative involvement in the issue of student unrest. Were the state legislators likely to take repressive measures in putting down student dissent? Did the demonstrations affect general legislation involving higher education? Were the schools which experienced student unrest likely to suffer in the legislature? Did the demonstrations affect appropriations for higher education?

None of these questions can be answered fully on the basis of this sample of legislative leaders alone. It was clear from our in-terviews, however, that while the student demonstrations had a predominantly negative effect on the legislators, those who would call for repressive measures or the reduction of expenditures for higher education were in the minority in all nine states when the survey was taken. But many officials warned that an increase in student unrest was likely to lead to legislative involvement—a warning which has since been followed by action in a number of states.

The amount of concern expressed varied from state to state and was not entirely related to the amount of unrest experienced by each state. Thus while California and New York had had the greatest amount of disruption, the legislators interviewed in these states were among the most tolerant. On the other hand, Texas, with relatively few demonstrations, appeared the most likely to respond with repressive measures. Officials from Kansas, Kentucky, and Iowa were largely undisturbed by the student disruptions—in part, at least, a reflection of the relative calm of their universities. The Louisiana legislators dismissed the unrest in their state, although these responses were probably not very indicative of how the state would react to continued disturbances in Negro colleges. Illinois and Pennsylvania officials were more upset by the demonstrations and warned of legislative action if the unrest were to increase.

California   This state, of course, stands as the birthplace of contemporary student unrest and as a continuing center of disturbance. And since the 1966 elections vested the governorship in a conservative Republican administration but the Legislature (at the time of the survey) in the control of the Democrats, the University became a major source of partisan controversy. Despite this apparent potential for legislative involvement in the student problems, California legislative leaders were fairly moderate. Only one was extremely hostile to the students; three others were among the more sympathetic legislators interviewed; and the remainder stressed the need to preserve academic freedom and freedom to dissent.

Some concern was expressed about the impact of the unrest on public and legislative support for higher education. A California Senator called it "the greatest single danger facing higher education today." He thought that once the schools became involved in political causes, the Legislature would have to create certain safeguards. A second official spelled out in detail how he thought the demonstrations might have an adverse effect upon the Legislature: they would make it less "amenable to increases in the budget," less "mindful of the needs for scholarships and assistance programs," and lead to the introduction of measures to keep certain activities off campus.

The Democrats interviewed, however, were less concerned about the effect of the students' activities on the Legislature than their effect on public opinion. One official noted that this was an election year. A second pointed out that "people are less upset over students riding in a clothes dryer than challenging the authority." In all, California legislators were less disturbed than might have been expected considering the extent of the disturbances and their involvement in partisan politics. There appeared to be less favor for legislative interference in the issue than in most other states with a similar amount of unrest.

Illinois   Here, respondents were divided rather sharply in their evaluations of student discord. About half were alarmed and called for greater discipline on the part of university officials. A 30-year veteran of the Assembly, for example, replied that the major problem facing higher education in the state was "student militancy, radicalism, disrespect"—which he saw as "just plain damn anarchy." Another thought that academic freedom was "just used as an excuse for flouting the law."

On the other hand, a number of officials believed that the students were frequently right in their grievances and should be listened to; they would let the universities take care of their own problems. "We have competent people running the University of Illinois," argued one Assemblyman. "If we don't like the board, we should get rid of them at the next election, but this is no problem for the legislators at all and we should stay out of it."

Both groups agreed, however, that while legislators frequently let themselves be influenced by the conduct of students, the unrest problem until then had been relatively slight in Illinois, with little impact on the Legislature. At the same time, many thought that legislative interference would be forthcoming if the student protests were to increase. A number of Illinois legislators had already called for some action, and a dispute over the recognition of the DuBois Club at the University of Illinois seemed to indicate some trend toward involvement. The trustees of the university decided to recognize the club as an official school organization, but changed their minds following a legislative resolution asking them to reconsider.

Iowa Legislators in Iowa were fairly open in their approach to the unrest although the state had experienced rather violent antiwar demonstrations and was conservative. Many appeared to be troubled by the demonstrations; none called for the outright dismissal of demonstrators. There did appear to be public pressure building up on the legislators, however. One Senator noted that he had to serve as an "interpreter" for all three state universities on the issue of unrest because others didn't want to become involved in it. He, along with two other officials, also reported a negative reaction on the part of many legislators in wanting to shut off funds to the universities. Such officials, one Senator asserted, were probably in the minority and probably wouldn't have voted for the appropriations in the first place. They were the ones who received the press, however, and they gave the Legislature a "black eye" by leaving the impression that it wasn't doing anything.

Kansas There were probably fewer student disruptions in Kansas than in any other state in the sample, and this fact was reflected in its legislators' reactions to the problem. None of the officials interviewed in this conservative Republican state was particularly upset by the student demonstrations, and none called for repressive measures either by the Legislature or the universities themselves. Most did indicate that the majority of the legislators reacted negatively to the demonstrations. One official asserted that the demonstrators hurt their own cause: "If the demonstrators had any concept of psychology, they would realize that they are working contrary to any point they want to make." While such a view would undoubtedly be shared by most Kansas legislators, those interviewed showed none of the emotional hostility found in many other states, and no legislator called for the dismissal of the student demonstrators or for legislative involvement.

Kentucky   This was another state which had experienced no large-scale student disruption at the time of the survey. A minor controversy did occur in 1968 over a scheduled University of Kentucky conference on the war and the draft. The conference turned out to be very critical of the Vietnam war. About 40 members of the House signed a resolution expressing the view that the university should not permit the conference to be held. The university president met with two sponsors of the resolution and convinced them the administration was doing a competent job of keeping student activities under control and that such a resolution would be harmful. The sponsors then decided not to introduce the resolution, and the conference was held without incident.

Most of the legislative leaders interviewed mentioned that conference. While most agreed with the president's handling of the situation, the majority noted that such activities had upset many legislators and would affect the level of support for higher education if they continued. One official said that the draft conference had influenced him to vote against a resolution to seat students on the board of trustees in a nonvoting capacity. A second noted that it was impossible to explain student actions to the average voter. A third was concerned about the conference undermining patriotism, and a fourth mentioned the "emotional factor" raised whenever the word *communism* was mentioned. There appeared, however, to be little urgency or alarm in these warnings. No Kentucky respondent called for the dismissal of students and none was among the extreme critics of the demonstrations.

One Assemblyman said that only 25 percent of the legislators were really concerned about student unrest. "But the ones that are," he asserted, "are a little like the students who want to create unrest. The numbers are small, but they make a lot of noise." A similar remark was made by a Senator concerning a bill to create a state un-American activities committee: "They're going to gripe about it and howl about it and make some nasty comments and speeches about it. But when it comes right down to going in and trying to find out and investigate it, they probably won't."

Louisiana On the whole, legislators in Louisiana appeared to be the most patronizing to the students. All those interviewed thought that the unrest was either a result of youthful rebellion or of bad advice on the part of professors and administrators. Two told stories about "uprisings" when they were in college, over trivial incidents involving a school rivalry and the adoption of a school mascot. One admitted to participating in a "bit of a lark" when he was in college. All thought that the universities had been too permissive and called for greater discipline; a few felt that harder work would serve as a deterrent to the unrest.

Since most disturbances in Louisiana had involved Negro schools (Southern University and Grambling College), the race issue undoubtedly affected the legislators' perceptions of the disorders.

New York Responses in New York were in some ways unique. A number of New York universities had recently been involved in a series of "pot busts"—a fact which was salient at the time and which disturbed a number of legislators. Thus, while most New York officials thought that student unrest would have an adverse effect on the Legislature, they generally appeared more worried about the illegal use of drugs on the state campuses than about student participation in political protests.* The following response of an Assemblyman was indicative of the degree of this concern:

This problem of drugs has caused a great deal of unrest among the legislators. They feel, "Don't tell me that school is loaded with nothing but drug addicts." Right away they think everybody is a drug addict, and they feel if that is going on, why should we worry about that school—close them up.

At the same time the New York legislators appeared more sophisticated than those in most other states and resisted simple solutions. Thus, while they were almost unanimous in indicating that

*The New York interviews, it should be noted, took place *before* the disturbances at Columbia University.

the student activities had a negative effect on the Legislature, none called for the Legislature to become involved in the problems on the state campuses. Rather, to the extent that such problems might adversely affect higher education, they thought them likely to slow down the state's expansion program:

Interviewer: Do you think the unrest on campuses has had an impact on your fellow legislators' willingness to support higher education?

Respondent: Definitely. This may be the excuse you hear. Let's be realistic about it. Those who are resisting the expansion — the expenditure — may well take this as a righteous indignation. A pot party is going on, and I guess I can't accept the new approach. I don't know what the new approach is; from what you read there certainly is a tremendous change in the mores today. Maybe this is good; I don't know. . . . As I was saying, I do think there has been a negative reaction — I'm very aware of it in the Assembly — to the orgies and the last bit they just had with reference to barring the recruiters and representatives from Dow.

Pennsylvania Legislators in Pennsylvania appeared more disturbed by the student disruptions than those in the other Northern states surveyed. There were no expressions of sympathy for the students — although most respondents saw no need for legislative involvement at that time. One official did note that the legislators must be responsive to the public and that the public was quite upset about demonstrations on tax-supported facilities.

Another Pennsylvania legislator was among the extreme reactionaries on the issue. "In our country," he argued, "our philosophy must be, if we're going to continue to exist, our country, right or wrong, still must be our country." He thought that the student demonstrations properly should affect appropriations:

I would certainly hope so. If a group of students is allowed to have their own way in this formative period when the taxpayers are making it possible for them to get a higher education, if they react against that, then they should have tougher punishment brought down on them.

While the majority of Pennsylvania officials interviewed were upset by the demonstrations, most would not yet call for legislative interference. If the unrest became more widespread, however, a number of officials thought that the Legislature would react negatively.

Texas The legislators in Texas were easily the most opinionated and divided of all we interviewed. Their responses included some of the most reactionary attacks on the students, as well as some of the most eloquent defenses of their conduct. It was fairly clear from the interviews, however, that the defenders were in the minority in the Legislature as a whole. The majority were disturbed by the unrest and favored a tough approach. One official, for example, praised the administration for taking a "hard line" position in expelling six students for demonstrating without a permit.

Another official attacked professors getting paid $15,000 a year while advocating the overthrow of government. "If the board of regents and the presidents of the college or university can't remove a person like that," he argued, "then I feel that the Legislature is going to take it in hand and do something about it." A third said that the use of police was "the only way to combat violence."

There thus appeared to be a willingness on the part of many to involve the Legislature. Most thought that there was no need for legislation at that time, but such a reaction appeared likely if the unrest became more widespread. Those who sympathized with the students were particularly disturbed by such a possibility. One such official indicated that "you are going to see much more reaction in the years ahead when the student demonstrations become more widespread and more severe." A second was even more pessimistic: "I think that you are going to see the board of regents given the power to expel students for unconventional behavior. I think you will see general regimentation of student behavior which is probably inconsistent with academic freedom."

Compared with the responses of legislators in other states, the Texas officials appeared hostile to the student activists and the most likely to meet such activism with repressive measures. In the previous session—before student demonstrations had taken on much significance in the state—the Legislature had passed and sent to the governor in a single day a bill permitting University of Texas police to carry arms.

LEGISLATORS UNDER PRESSURE Our responses indicated, then, that a large proportion of the legislative leaders in the nine states were upset by student unrest, thought the universities should be less permissive in their handling of demonstrators, and felt that continued disruptions would lead to legislative involvement in the issue. A few such officials— certainly the most vocal ones—fit the image of the conservative reactionary who would like nothing better than to put the university in its place. The overwhelming majority, however, considered themselves sympathetic to higher education and understanding of its needs. Most gave serious consideration to the causes of the discontent, and many thought that the activists' cases had merit and should be heard.

Since the survey was composed of party leaders and members who served on committees that handled legislation dealing with education, such sympathy perhaps should have been expected. Further, many officials pointed out that they themselves were university graduates and thus had some understanding of the problems the universities were experiencing. Why, then, were so many legislators disturbed by the demonstrations and why did so many predict that further unrest might lead to legislative action?

In part, at least, the answer was political. The student demonstrations were not, after all, carried on in a vacuum but were related to issues which divided politicians as well as the general public. This fact was brought out by the Louisiana legislator who wished the universities would have more speakers who were concerned with "constitutional government"; by the Texas official who would not censor the school newspaper as long as its editors were "reasonable" and didn't advocate "overthrow" and "some of this radical stuff we hear"; as well as by the Illinois legislator who was tired of hearing what was wrong with the country. If the universities themselves became involved in issues affecting and dividing politicians, in other words, they should expect to be distrusted by those officials who found themselves on the other side.

A Senator from California—where the political dimensions of the demonstrations had perhaps been most acute—warned against the political involvement of the universities. His statement deserves to be quoted in length:

Up until now the institution of higher learning has been regarded as an isolated island . . . where the tradition of what we call academic freedom has been studiously observed, and the Legislature and the governor have tried to . . . observe it. Now you face the situation where these institutions become staging areas, if you like, for rather extensive experiments in social change and aggressive movements out in the community, off the island.

And once they do that—and they've already done it—they then force the government on every level to redefine their relationship to the institution.

As a legislator, I have to, above all, be conscious of and sensitive to the feelings of the people I represent. And it's when the students and the faculty themselves . . . leave the campus to carry their crusades to the community in terms of overaction that they then force us to react . . . and jeopardize the traditional role of the institution. . . . As they move to make the institution a politically powerful unit or a unit that can be used to political advance, they force us to build certain safeguards against that utilization. And these safeguards . . . erode the function of the institution.

To the extent that the university—whether by design or accident —became a political force in itself, it was likely to make enemies among some politicians and members of the public. More important, perhaps, the general public was not as tolerant of academic idiosyncracies as the predominantly university-educated state legislators. If the politicians heard anything from their constituents about higher education, as shown above, it was likely to be complaints about demonstrators, hippies, and those who burned draft cards. Most communications, in short, came from those who were not well educated and were hostile to the universities, who worried about how their tax money was spent rather than whether a quality education was provided. Such a group, as one Californian pointed out, "is predominant in our society—those are the ones who are paying most of the bills."

Thus the general public was less likely to understand the need for academic freedom in the university and more likely to react negatively to the use of tax money for anything other than strictly educational purposes. It would be surprising if such a public did not call for the dismissal of those who refused to conform to the norms. A few legislators indicated this was already the case: "People feel that it is a privilege to go to the school and not a right." "There is a limit to how much the public can stand for in the name of academic freedom." Others said it was impossible to explain the need for academic freedom to the average individual.

"There is no way that you can justify it to John Jones down at the corner store," said a Kentucky Senator. "You can't talk to him about academic freedom or the necessity of freedom of speech . . . he doesn't understand it and there's no need to even try to explain it." A Pennsylvania Assemblyman thought that the typical response of the public was to take punitive actions against those who protested. A Texan indicated that people in his state favored the use of police and troops to settle the demonstrations.

Not only were a number of the legislators themselves distrustful of the actions of the dissident students and faculty, but they were often under intense pressure from the public to take strong actions to end the demonstrations. The result was that those who might have defended the activists found it politically dangerous to do so. A New York legislator noted that public pressure forced some officials to "make public utterances that they don't even feel privately. They overact because they have to keep in touch with their constituency which is a hell of a lot broader."

It was difficult to tell, in conclusion, how much these warnings represented the desire of respondents for the protesters to deescalate their activities and thus reduce the conflict experienced by the politician. It was obvious that many liberal officials felt politically uncomfortable, caught between their desire to support higher education and their desire to remain in office. Such a dilemma may explain the almost unanimous belief that the universities themselves should exercise greater discipline over the dissident students.

These interviews suggested, however, that the demonstrations forced many legislators to consider the issues raised by the students. Up until the spring riots of 1968, furthermore, the activists appeared to have gained the sympathy, if not the support, of a fairly large number of state officials. The warning that increased disorders would result in greater public disenchantment and legislative reappraisal and/or reprisal apparently has since come to pass in many areas of the country. Student activism is, as many politicians predicted, rapidly becoming a political issue.

9. The University
and Society

One of the most frequent causes of conflict in academia lies in the multiplicity of services which higher education is expected to provide. Universities, it is commonly held, exist not just to educate students but to help solve the community's social, economic, and political problems as well. They must provide expert advice and research for government, train employees for their states' industries and businesses, and engage in the social and economic affairs of their own communities. Not infrequently, of course, such goals are in conflict.

In part, conflict results from the diverse constituencies which public institutions of higher education must satisfy. Internally, the school's administration, faculty, and students may have different conceptions of the proper duties of the institution. Externally, the general public, the school's governing board, and the state's legislative and executive officials will often make conflicting demands. Even without these diverse sources of expectations, of course, the modern university would experience frequent conflicts in goals. Such common areas as admissions, expansion, and hiring are all influenced by the way authorities define the role of higher education and its relation to other societal goals. The university, in other words, must consider itself as a social and economic agent as well as a center of knowledge and education.

A number of questions in the interview dealt with various functions which the university might be expected to perform, and legislator's responses to these questions—the provision of universal public education, aid to minority and low-income groups, urban assistance, and professional training—are summarized in this chapter. We also asked about the university's effects on the state's economy. The respondents' positions on the first three of these issues, it was found, generally lacked any clear patterns. A high consensus existed in the other two subjects. Virtually all officials indicated that there was a shortage of doctors and teachers in their states and that higher education had a highly beneficial impact upon their states' economy and welfare.

UNIVERSAL PUBLIC EDUCATION
A question which probed the role of service in a very general sense concerned universal public education. "Would you say," the respondents were asked, "that everyone is entitled to a college education at public expense?" Only a few officials unconditionally endorsed universal public education; the majority either disapproved of this notion or gave qualified responses. Some did not think that all students were capable of obtaining a higher education or that the state was obligated to pay for it; others said such an education should be provided only for those who had the necessary "desire" or "ability." There was considerable sentiment for students to make some effort toward paying for their own education.

Legislators who favored universal public education were primarily from the largest states—Texas, California, and New York. Typical arguments in support of this proposal were "The state owes it to individuals," "Society would benefit from everybody being educated," and "Higher education is necessary in this day and age." A New York Assemblyman, for example, said, "Everyone who desires it should be given the opportunity. Both the state and federal government owe that obligation." A California Senator believed that the nation itself would benefit from such a program, and added: "I don't think that everybody would end up going to college because some people are obviously not going to go. But for those who want to go, there should be an opportunity." A Texas legislator thought everyone entitled to at least a junior college education.

The word "opportunity" entered into the responses of a number of officials. They felt that everybody should be provided an opportunity to attend college—although not necessarily at state expense. As one official put it: "I will say that I think every student in this state who wants to go to college should have the opportunity. I didn't say free." Another commented:

I said at the beginning that I didn't think the state necessarily should furnish everyone with a college education. I think it's the obligation of the state to furnish every boy and girl an opportunity to get an education. But I think they should do it and must do it on their own initiative.

A Kansas Assemblyman indicated that the policy of his state was to admit all high school graduates and allow the students to find out whether they could carry the work. "It is an expensive system, a cumbersome system," he said, "but it is a system that we Kansans have chosen and I think it is proper to continue it."

About a dozen officials felt that higher education should be made available to those who had the "ability" or "desire." Two typical responses follow—the first by a Senator from New York, the second by a Kentucky Senator:

. . . everyone who has the desire and the ability. And the two go together. I think the question of abilities is a very difficult one to solve. Again, it is a mixture of motivation, ability, and previous training. . . . But the area of opportunity lies in higher education in our society. You cannot make it in our society . . . unless you have gone to college.

Yes, so far as they're able, they're entitled. I certainly know—and I think most people would realize—that every person won't get a college education, and it might be a bad thing if some of them did do this, but I think they're entitled to it . . . if they have the ability and the desire, why then I think they should be entitled to it, yes.

How to determine who had the ability and desire to attend college and who didn't was a question which these respondents admittedly could not solve. A number of them, as indicated above, felt that junior colleges could play such a screening role.

About 10 respondents simply said that not everyone was entitled to a college education at public expense. Their reasons varied but financial considerations frequently entered into their calculations. "I think that this would be a good utopia," a Texas Assemblyman replied, "but I don't think that we can effectively afford it." A Kentucky Senator similarly felt that if such a program were put into practice, private business "would reach the point where its facilities would be taxed to the limit." He thought the state had a duty to educate only a "reasonable number" of students. A Pennsylvania Assemblyman took a similar position. "I cannot say that everyone is qualified [for] a college education at public expense," he said. "The determination of who is qualified is a university matter."

A final group of respondents preferred a system in which students themselves contributed something toward the financing of their education. Many thought that students would get more out of their education if they helped pay for it. A Texas legislator contrasted the salaries of legislators with student scholarships:

I feel a little about that like I do about legislative salaries. There is a balance at some point. I would hate to see a legislator seek the office because it was a place for him to work and for his family to be comfortable. I would hate to think that we were setting something up as such that a person had a place where he could be safe from society and its burdens and responsibilities until he was 21 and a graduate at public expense.

He indicated that a loan program ought to be established so the student himself would have to make some effort. A similar position was taken by a Pennsylvania official:

I would place the burden of repaying on each one who would secure the benefits of higher education. Through that method I think they will get much more out of it. The other day at an educational conference one man spoke up and said he had sweated blood to get a little education on his own and now he's sweating blood to get an education for his boy and girl and he believed that that was wrong—that the boy and girl should be doing their own sweating.

AID TO MINORITY AND LOW-INCOME GROUPS Because education is often viewed as a major means of advancement in this country, many individuals have argued that public colleges and universities should make special efforts to assist the members of minority and low-income groups. The state officials' opinions on this matter varied widely. While the majority approved of such programs in principle, there seemed to be little consensus on how they should be carried out. The largest single group of respondents, in fact, asserted that extra efforts were better directed at elementary or secondary education than at college-age students.

Officials responding favorably to the inquiry offered a variety of possible means by which to help minority groups and individuals from poor families. These included job training, public or private loans and scholarships, and the lowering of admission standards for certain individuals. New York officials were particularly enthusiastic about their own program for the disadvantaged student (SEEK). "I think the SEEK program is an excellent one," replied one such respondent. "Wonderful. It is unfortunate that it cannot be expanded further or faster." A second New York legislator linked education with employment, which he saw as the major need of minority groups.

A number of state leaders were critical of admission standards which often screened out members of culturally or otherwise disadvantaged groups and advocated less arbitrary criteria for such individuals. A California Senator, for example, felt that many Mexican-Americans in his district were losing out because their cultural and language disadvantages placed them just below the cutoff point. "I don't think we have to be quite so severe as we are sometimes by holding right to that line," he argued. Another legislator, himself a Negro, was strongly critical of the testing program used for admissions in his state. "The original concept of testing," he asserted, "was not designed to accommodate people whose cultural background differs from the advantaged citizen." He also criticized the manner in which individuals obtaining low test scores were allowed special admissions in his state. "Check the statistics," he said, "and you find that more than 50 percent of those students are athletes. Now they might be black athletes, they might be Mexican-American athletes—but they still are not using that 2 percent flexibility for disadvantaged students."

A number of officials who were sympathetic to this general argument placed greater emphasis on special programs in the primary and secondary schools. A New York Assemblyman believed that more opportunities should be provided "at a lower level so when it comes time for college they can start on an even keel with everyone else." A Texan said:

I think that we need to do a lot more on the primary education level and the secondary education level to see that minority groups provide us with students who can do college work. . . . We are a long way off from offering equal opportunity in higher education, but I don't know that it is anything which can be corrected now in higher education. It is something which has to be corrected in kindergarten and grades 1 to 12.

A Pennsylvanian similarly thought that the problem was in the lower grades. "Our system of society," he said, "whatever it is, has placed a great majority of these people in circumstances that they can't move themselves up to get ready to go to college."

Those who opposed programs to assist minority groups nearly all argued that membership in a minority group did not carry a right to special privileges. Representative of this viewpoint was the following response from an Illinois legislator:

Yes, I think that special efforts should be made to encourage them to do it and to help them in every way possible. But I don't think that they should be given advantages just because they are a minority group or because they are underprivileged people.

A few other officials took the position that, as one put it, "Anybody in Pennsylvania or in America who is determined to get an education will get that." A Kentucky and a Texas legislator, respectively, claimed:

I don't know of any qualified young man or woman who wants a college education that can't get one . . . and if they can't raise the small tuition, we have, for example, at home our Rotary Club has loans which will be extended to them if they are qualified and can be paid back after they get out. That's true all over Kentucky.

Programs that we have now are probably adequate. In my area I have never had a Negro boy or girl up to this point . . . come to my attention who wanted to go to college where I couldn't get them a loan or scholarship so that they could go to college. I have never had a single case of anyone who came to me from a low-income minority group and [said] that they wanted to go to college that I was unable to get them a loan or scholarship to provide enough money for them to go.

URBAN EXTENSION CENTERS Public universities have assisted farmers through agricultural extension centers for the past 50 years. A possible avenue of assistance to areas of poverty, it would appear, is the adoption of similar centers in urban areas. When the state officials were asked their opinions on this matter, however, most had little knowledge or conception of what such a service would be. At the same time, those who did respond were generally favorable to some efforts in this area, indicating legislative approval of such programs might be forthcoming in the future.

The state leaders giving positive responses felt that extension centers would be valuable in helping urban areas solve their unique problems. They often emphasized different services that such centers could provide. A New York Assemblyman asserted:

I think if higher education got its proper force behind it, some of our urban problems wouldn't be as severe as they are. I think we have to admit that education is one of the core problems of urban unrest. . . . What ought to be done is to offer youngsters more opportunity to go to higher education. . . . They ought to have some vocational training if they are not geared for professional type schools.

A New York Assemblywoman emphasized the expert information which such centers could provide poor families in New York:

We have here at Cornell this excellent faculty and excellent source of information on problems of very direct relevance to the poverty families in the cities. The idea is to try to work out the same thing from the home economics college to the poverty-stricken mother in the central part of New York City.

A Texas legislator felt that the expansion of universities in the cities would help the economic development of those areas. "When you get more colleges and universities in your urban areas," he said, "then you're going to get graduate schools in conjunction . . . and then you're going to create the talent that's necessary for the economy of that area." An Illinois administrator strongly endorsed university programs oriented toward urban problems and complained that the schools were not doing enough:

Well, there are programs developing in, I think, most of the major institutions. I don't think there's any question about this. All of them have centers for urban affairs which were nonexistent five years ago. All of them are paying increasing attention to urban problems. But I can't say that there is any one of them—and I include both public and private institutions—any one of them that looks upon public service as their primary function or that has reallocated its resources in such a way that it would look as if they're shifting in this direction.

He felt that the recently opened campus in Chicago—located in the heart of the ghetto area—had not met the needs of its urban environment:

Two million Negroes within about a mile, up to two, three, four miles away, and yet less than 3 percent of its enrollment is Negro. . . . It doesn't somehow meet the kind of need, I think, that we have in that kind of urban environment. It's very difficult to meet those needs, but I think that we have to create institutions or create a new thrust in order to meet that kind of demand and so far we haven't done it.

Such responses, it should be repeated, were in the minority. Most state officials had little information about such centers and thus had not developed clear opinions as to their need or possible functions.

MEETING THE STATES' PROFESSIONAL NEEDS A more clear-cut response pattern emerged to questions concerning the states' professional needs. Almost all the officials indicated there was a shortage of doctors and teachers in their states. Some thought that their states could use more lawyers or veterinarians as well, but the need for doctors and teachers was primary.

Typical comments: "We're very short of doctors. We need more medical schools" (Pennsylvania). "We need more dentists, doctors, and other professional people — even veterinarians" (Texas). "Rural Iowa is screaming for lack of doctors" (Iowa). "I don't think we are producing . . . doctors and people in the health sciences as masterfully as we should be" (California). "Certainly any time you take a look at the rising cost of medical care and the rising need, you know we aren't turning out doctors and doctors' assistants fast enough to meet the need" (New York).

Similar, although less urgent, comments were made about teachers. Some differences of opinion existed, however, concerning the causes of the teacher shortage. Some officials thought that facilities were adequate but that incentives had to be raised to attract more individuals into the profession; others blamed the shortage primarily upon antiquated methods of instruction and accreditation. Respondents from California, Illinois, Iowa, and New York, respectively, said:

We don't have enough teachers. We have to provide incentives. . . . We need to provide more incentives for teachers because there is a critical shortage, especially in the urban areas.

There's a shortage of teachers. As far as I know, all who want to go into teacher training are able to, so we don't need more facilities.

It's a lack of interest. . . . I understand in this state we're going to be very short of teachers this coming year. Teaching . . . doesn't compare yet financially with some of the other vocations. . . . But I don't know just how we can change the desire of young people to be something else rather than teachers.

There is a need and a demand for more teachers. . . . I suppose the solution is to make the career of teaching attractive enough to motivate people to get into it.

Those who criticized the teacher-training programs thought that they were outdated and did not adjust to the needs of the local community. A California legislator gave an example of how such programs, by failing to prepare the individual to teach in certain areas, led to frustrations:

I think we have to devise some new courses for teaching disadvantaged students. You and I go to school and we go to teacher training, and you are the real outstanding teacher and I am the terrible teacher. They send me up to suburbia, and the children make me look good. I end up as the principal of that school. You go to the ghetto, the barrio, and you just can't cope with the peculiar problems there, and you're looking bad and you get a job at Douglas Aircraft.

HIGHER EDUCATION AND ECONOMIC DEVELOPMENT

A final service of the universities explored in the interviews was the contribution of higher education to economic development. Virtually all state officials believed higher education was positively linked to their states' economic and social well-being. The most common response was that colleges and universities attracted industry—both because of the technical expertise of faculty and because they trained students for employment. Less frequently mentioned was the role of higher education in alleviating social problems, but those who considered this function were again positive in their assessments. A few officials remarked that higher education could help cope with problems of increasing leisure or could supply more faculty and more educated persons to participate in public affairs.

Legislators who positively linked higher education to economic progress were found in all nine states in the survey. Some of the more typical responses follow.

An Illinois Senator:

Higher education is directly associated with economic development. The corporate institutions and the farms and the professional people. The training for these people benefits the state. All of these benefit from it.

A California official:

Of course higher education has an effect on the economic development and welfare of California. That's one of the reasons we've done so well. And this is the reason why I said earlier that I am not for imposing heavy tuition on the graduate student. It's a cinch we could hold onto him here. He makes a contribution to the state.

A New York legislator:

I think right now higher education is absolutely crucial . . . just look at Ithaca. Just what would it be without higher education? Actually our education has been a major factor in attracting and holding industry in this state. . . . We are one of the few states which has done this successfully.

A Kansas Senator:

I think you can't have substantial or effective economic development in this state without it being coordinated with our higher educational effort. . . . The really significant economic development is going to grow in this state in a corridor from Manhattan to Kansas City. And it is directly related to the institutions of higher education and the programs at the universities.

A Pennsylvania Senator:

I think the very fine medical facilities in and around the city of Philadelphia have definitely stimulated the economy of Pennsylvania. I think that more could be done. . . . If we had 10 times as many people going for Ph.D.'s and getting them in Pennsylvania, I think definitely it would improve the economy.

And a Texas Assemblyman:

Oh, well, certainly, higher education has had a great impact — a very satisfactory impact. And I think that the many institutions of higher education . . . have contributed greatly to . . . the general advance, the general increase of industrial development. I will give you one example. In 1963 we approved . . . making San Angelo Junior College a four-year school. . . . And since San Angelo has been made a senior college, I understand that it has been responsible for 14 or 15 new industries locating in that particular area.

Several respondents explained that a well-developed system of higher education attracted industry because of the greater number of skilled people produced. A Texas Representative, asked how more could be done to stimulate Texas' economy, replied:

Well, training people. In other words, having adequate higher educational facilities regardless of whether it be purely academic or vocational-technical or whatever. . . . I think that is the first thing that any industry is going to look for — what kind of training you have. . . . I think that one of the greatest assets that we have now or have ever had is the system of junior colleges that we are advancing. . . . I think that it will attract new industry to Texas. . . . [By state law] there cannot be a new junior college established unless they set up a vocational and technical department. And that looks good to industry.

An Iowa Senator similarly declared:

I think that this has been one of our great assets in Iowa . . . our schools and the people that we've made available for industry and professional businesses. I think this is what gives Iowa the good name we've had in . . . all the states — the product that we've put out of our institutions.

Several state leaders wanted to see more scientifically oriented programs in their universities in order to attract more industry. The most articulate of these was a Texas respondent who wanted the University of Houston to become involved in space research:

Many industries go to the area which trains research scientists and where you have universities to conduct substantial research. California, I think, is of course the classic example of this. They have had the research facilities and the research personnel, and industries go there because they can get a lot of free work done for them in their research departments. I think that we have a lot of opportunity in that area. Take the University of Houston. It is the university which ought to go into your space research since NASA is right there, and you've got the finest brains in the world in that field right in Houston itself or in the suburbs.

A Senator from New York thought that his state was behind in this respect because "we have not provided the talent on the spot."

Several legislators worried that not enough trained people were staying in the state where they had been educated or that not enough were being produced in a state. A Representative from Pennsylvania said:

I don't think [education] has really helped us economically as yet. I think we're still a state that is exporting its youth. We don't want to export them but they're leaving on their own. We're still a state of iron, steel, coal, rails. Here in Pennsylvania we've missed the automotive industry, we've missed the aircraft industry, we've missed the missile industry. . . . I don't know what the next great field is that is coming along, but if we don't latch onto that, we're going to go along another generation or two. . . . As far as I can tell, we're just giving a general, broad liberal arts education, which is fine and is nice for everyone to have. That means our people can leave and go to California and join the aircraft industry; they can go to Florida and join the missile industry; they can go to Michigan and join the automotive industry. . . . We're supplying doctors and psychiatrists from Philadelphia for the world.

Several legislators linked social as well as economic well-being with the development of higher education in their states. A New York committee chairman cited the great economic and social benefits realized from educating underprivileged and minority groups — helping them to become "productive members of society":

The more productive people you have, the more it increases your gross product, which filters to all. Obviously, with an educated society you have less problems in all areas — health, crime, welfare. It just raises the level, I think.

A member of the Pennsylvania Assembly said:

The whole process of higher education has an immediate impact on the welfare of the state. For instance, take the Negro. The Negro people at the present time are the ones who drain the heaviest on the state treasury for such things as public assistance for housing. . . . To make these people self-sustaining, to make them tax ratable, to cut down the drain, in turn, on the state treasury can only come about as a result of their being educated, to be able to be employed and bring home a decent salary, to become property owners so they can pay their fair share of property taxes.

A Texas Senator who also acknowledged the tremendous potential social benefits of higher education maintained that Texas had not yet made much progress in this respect:

Higher education has never really reached down and lifted up kids who really need a post-high school program. Higher education in Texas has always been sort of business oriented. . . . That has been its major impact, but on the other jobs of higher education, say taking kids from low income groups and giving them a chance to get ahead, it hasn't ever done very well.

A California Senator declared:

One of our problems is leisure time. We're going towards the 20-hour workweek someday in California. We're going to have leisure time on our hands, and the question is how are people going to use it? . . . I think that higher education, and particularly the junior college, is a place where this can be done. . . . We have to get people interested . . . the people who are going to do painting and basket-weaving, and community theater work; the people who are going to travel, do things in nature, do things in the humanities; giving their time to projects that have humanitarian effect—this has a very definite effect, and I think the greatest slant should be here, towards what people will do with their time.

A New York Assemblyman commented:

The big contribution educational institutions could make is to permit their faculties to participate in state government. I have found it is very difficult to get men from the schools to participate in our research work. . . . I think if the schools permitted their faculty to participate in our committee work and our committee structure and our research, I think you'll find that out of it comes better legislation, too. By getting better legislation, you create more avenues for stimulus in the growth of our economy; this is what we ought to be looking for.

CONCLUSION There is a high consensus on the university's economic role in the state but disagreement over its role as an agent of social change or racial equality. Virtually all officials agreed that the universities were and should be linked to attracting industry to their states and to providing professional expertise. They were divided, however, over whether they should promote social equality by providing free education for all and by making special efforts to assist individuals from minority groups, poor families, or urban areas. Their disagreement in these latter cases existed on both the principles involved and the means to effectuate change. Thus there was more unanimity over the university's role in the states' economies than in solving social problems.

10. *Planning and the Future*

Public policy is a subtle blend of past experience, present conditions, and expectations of the future. It is generally recognized that the past constrains the present and the present constrains the future. That expectations of the future constrain the present involves a conception of the policy process that is both more difficult to fathom and to prove. This is particularly true in the case of policy-making bodies such as legislatures whose members, being elected, are more likely to respond to current pressures than to demands that may be made on them in the distant future.

Planning—letting present policies be influenced by future goals and proposals for their implementation—is not a characteristic feature of legislative decision making. Yet, insofar as planning does enter public policy making, images of the future are relevant and possibly decisive. If these images are unduly optimistic or unduly pessimistic, the plan is likely to be unrealistic and the process of implementing it inconsistent and confused. How politicians view the future is, therefore, a critical variable in any arena of public policy in which planning for the future is recognized as an essential component of the policy-making process.

THE ISSUE OF A MASTER PLAN Of the nine states included in the survey, three—California, Illinois, and New York—had more or less well-established master plans for higher education. One state, Pennsylvania, had a new and quite untried plan; Texas was evolving a plan; and in four states—Iowa, Kansas, Kentucky, and Louisiana—master planning was not practiced. Our question about master planning was not asked in all nine states; but, fortunately, it was asked in two states with a master plan, in a state just beginning master planning, and in two states with no plans.* Because of the quite distinct interstate differences in response patterns, we shall present the material state by state. As will appear, Californians seemed less satisfied with the implementation of their plan than were legislators in Illinois. The Pennsylvania respondents were generally pleased, although they felt there had not been enough experience with the plan to make a judgment. Most Iowans thought it sounded like a good idea to have some sort of long-range plan, but Kansas respondents were generally more reluctant to endorse the concept of master planning for higher education.

California Californians, though approving of the idea of a master plan, complained that the existing plan (initiated in 1960) had not satisfactorily defined the different roles of and relationships among the University, state colleges, and junior colleges. Many indicated that the plan had intensified conflicts and dissatisfaction among educational institutions. Their complaints suggested that a master plan is not necessarily the cure-all to problems such as interinstitutional competition, nor is it the unmixed blessing that some legislators in states without such a plan might anticipate. Most Californians considered their plan out of date and in serious need of reevaluation and revision. One legislator declared: "Once conceived here [the master plan] fit that time. But we need to have a new master plan. I'm hopeful that the Joint Committee on Higher Education will come up with something."

A high-ranking member of the Joint Legislative Committee on Higher Education predicted a revamping of the master plan:

The master plan was somewhat of a holding action . . . to discourage some sorts of obvious competition and friction among the segments [of higher education] for a period of years when new institutions were being developed. It managed to hold down that friction. But in the last three or four years . . . education has been developing some very serious problems. . . . The state colleges as a system are no longer willing to accept the status which they did accept in the master plan. The junior colleges are developing into a different type of system [than the plan anticipated]. . . . The coordinating council [established by the plan] has developed largely as a

*In the states with a master plan the question was "Are you satisfied with the way in which the master plan has worked in the state?" In the states without a master plan the wording was "Do you think a master plan for higher education should be developed?"

useless body in respect to serious problems in higher education. . . . [It] seems to me that a whole brand-new type of administration and governance is going to have to be developed, and the master plan doesn't provide for that.

Another Californian thought that a basic problem in creating an effective master plan was the differing perceptions which legislators and educators held of the state colleges:

We have gone along on the assumption that the master plan . . . would control the development of higher education in the state. And yet the perception of the master plan and the role of the state colleges in the master plan is far different on the legislative level than it is on the academic level back at the institution. . . . [The legislators] assumed as a result of the master plan that the state college would act basically as an instructing type of institution . . . and have a role somewhat equated to the teacher preparation college. . . . We tend to interpret the master plan as intending that the state college has to fulfill a separate function from the University.

He proposed that any revised plan "give back to the individual campuses greater flexibility and control over budget and expenditures . . . and over some other decisions as well."

Illinois In contrast to the California legislators, those from Illinois seemed generally satisfied with their master plan. For instance, an important member of the House Committee on Higher Education remarked:

Yes, as far as I can see [the master plan] is working reasonably well. I think it's an obvious step forward to have somebody thinking about the future. This is real important, particularly in a growing field like higher education. And the board, I think, has done a good job in projecting numbers, for example, in just that one simple area, in planning where other colleges should go. Their plans were for four more colleges, but we only have two of them coming up this round.

A Senator thought that the master plan was "outstanding," and seemed pleased with the Illinois Board of Higher Education. Another legislator was somewhat more reserved in his approval:

Well, I would have to say . . . yes. I'm not satisfied with all of the things that have been done, but the master plan—we had to have something. We had to have something to coordinate all this, and I would have to say I was satisfied, although I think with hindsight that we might do better in certain areas than we have.

Another Senator thought the master plan was "going all right," but that "it's too early" to make a definite appraisal. And another Senator felt that, although the master plan was working well enough, lack of money might slow it down:

Yes, I think we may find . . . with the financial pinch that I see coming very soon in the next biennium, we may find we have to slow it down a little bit, but I think it has worked. We've made some changes in it. We increased the state's scholarships, for example, last year. I think generally it has worked very well.

Pennsylvania Pennsylvania passed a bill for a master plan a little over a year before the time of our interviews. Most legislators in this state were of the opinion that not enough of the plan had been implemented to make it truly effective or to evaluate it properly. The most positive evaluation of the effectiveness of the plan came from the legislator who said:

You have to remember that the master plan is rather new. And I think that if you go back over the master plan you would be amazed in how many of the recommendations have been implemented at the present time. You'll find that some of these have been implemented by executive action. For example, the Department of Public Instruction has been reorganized. You'll find that we are making tremendous advances in our scholarship program.

Most Pennsylvanians were a bit more reserved in their approval. One thought that the master plan could "stand considerable refinement." Others expressed dislike of certain aspects of the plan. Said one: "It looks good on paper, but I'm not satisfied with the way we are meeting what used to be called the 'extension problem.'" And several anticipated problems of implementation. One Senator reported that legislation in violation of the intent of the plan was being passed:

A good example, last week we passed a bill that ran counter to the master plan. . . . Penn State Extension in Delaware County. I initially started out against the thing, but I finally said something has to get off that Senate here. So I ended up voting for the darned thing, even though if the master plan does ever get off the ground this won't necessarily fit into the scheme of the master plan. But at the rate we're going we may never see this enabling legislation.

Kansas   Kansas has no master plan, and the legislators who were asked about the desirability of having one varied in their opinions from being interested to opposing the idea. One commented:

It might be a good thing. Our system works pretty well. We have always had a good board of regents. We have always had the highest type of citizens sitting on the board. Of course they do a great deal of long-range planning. I suppose they have never done what formally could be called a master plan. I don't know what kind of personnel you would need to prepare that kind of a plan. Yes, I think generally it would be a desirable thing.

Another Senator said: "Our board of regents does plan down the road, for about 10 years at a time. Each school has a plan as to its growth. I do not see a real pressing need for a master plan, but it might be desirable."
And a high-ranking member of an education committee commented: "Oh, it could be desirable. . . . We have very proud alumni associations which act frequently to the detriment of higher education. The individual alumnus in the House or Senate tends to protect his own alma mater."
   Other legislators were somewhat skeptical of the value of a master plan. A member of the Education Committee cautioned:

Well, planning is always useful and so I suppose it is a good idea. But I think planning has got to be flexible so we can adjust to meet actual needs. I think the people involved in higher education themselves are the best ones to decide for the future. So any plan ought to be flexible and not rigid—something people can work from, and it should come from the people involved.

A colleague declared:

I don't think it can be [formalized in a general master plan]. I think you have to remain somewhat flexible. I think you need a plan as a general guide, but you can't formalize it too much. I just came from the subcommittee of the Ways and Means Committee where we are reviewing the supplemental budgets for this current fiscal year [for higher education]. We had some drastic changes in anticipated revenue from tuition and fees and in anticipated enrollments. We have these every year. . . . Try as you will . . . you can't predict accurately what is going to happen.

A few Kansans distinctly opposed the creation of a master plan— generally on the grounds that it was "unnecessary" or would create too much centralized control over education.

Iowa In contrast to most Kansans, Iowa legislators tended to approve the creation of a master plan. One leader, emphatically in favor, noted that plans for one were already being made:

I think that the wheels are already turning for such a plan. . . . I certainly hope that they will come up with a report that will be translated into a plan. . . . We've pushed pretty hard to get the regents to think of long-range planning. . . . This is an era of planning . . . we must have long-range planning.

A member of the House Education Committee anticipated that a master plan would soon be developed. He approved whole-heartedly: "Master planning is not new to me . . . and I'm much appalled with the state of Iowa because we have no long-range planning for any agency in government. . . . I think we need to know where we're actually going." Other Iowans, though endorsing the idea of a master plan, stressed the need for "flexibility" and for keeping "politics" out of the planning process. A member of the House told the interviewer:

I think that it would definitely, probably . . . be helpful. But I tend to be just a little bit skeptical of master plans particularly if they are very detailed. A general view and policy type of approach would be beneficial, but a detailed master plan where you're going to build the next building 14 years from now and that sort of thing is probably not going to get much attention paid to it. . . . [I would like to see] one that could be reviewed periodically and updated, and we could tell whether some of the general guidelines had been followed, and if they had, whether the enrollments, demands, or so forth, came out as expected.

Another legislator declared: "Oh, certainly, it's desirable to have a plan of some kind. The problem always is, though, of course, who draws the plan and what are their motives. And any plan you have has got to be flexible." And a third commented: "A master plan would be fine if whoever set it up would do it on a constructive basis and not have it loaded in any way in favor of one particular group or the other."

THE FUTURE: SHORT VIEW In order to elicit state officials' views of what the future of higher education might look like in their states, they were asked two general questions—one concerning "the next few years" and another concerning the more distant future. As might be expected, the distant future was more dimly seen than more immediate developments.

The great majority in all nine states agreed that enrollment was going to increase in coming years, although some predicted a larger increase than others, and a few thought that demand would level off. For instance, a Louisiana legislator anticipated "probably a 5 or 6 percent increase per year," while an Iowa respondent thought that enrollments would continue to rise until three-fourths of the young people in his state had the opportunity to get a higher education. A Pennsylvanian declared: "No one in his right mind would say that the demand for higher education is going to decrease. We'll have to use all of our facilities." And several respondents, like the following Assemblyman from Illinois, said estimates were too conservative: "I get these estimates done by college people all the time, and they are invariably conservative."

But others felt that enrollment increases would not be a major problem over the next few years. Several attributed an expected leveling off of enrollment to a declining birth rate.

Some of the respondents anticipating increases specified such reasons as greater demand for higher education on the part of minority group students, the growth of community colleges, the need for technical and vocational skills, more graduate education, draft deferments, general economic affluence, and simply the desire to have a degree.

RECOMMENDATIONS FOR MEETING DEMAND The state officials were asked how they thought their state could best meet the increasing demand for higher education. Should existing public facilities be enlarged? Should new facilities be created? Should the junior colleges be increased? Should more use be made of the private schools?

Few respondents gave top priority to creating new campuses. This was not surprising. Budget-conscious legislators viewed new campuses as the most expensive means of coping with rising enrollments. Most preferred expansion of existing facilities, especially of junior colleges. But in spite of favoring enlargement of existing campuses, many respondents also noted that problems were inherent in the development of very large institutions and cautioned that there were limits beyond which schools could not or should not grow.

If new institutions were to be built, most legislators favored what they regarded as the most economical type of institution—the junior college. A few suggested more urban campuses, and extension programs were mentioned. Several suggested that the need for enlarging campuses and creating new facilities could be partly alleviated by more efficient use of existing facilities—specifically through the specialization of programs and statewide coordination of curricula.

EXPANSION OF FACILITIES Several leaders gave fairly general replies to our questions on how to best meet the increasing demand for higher education, stating simply that all higher educational facilities should be expanded. A Pennsylvania committee chairman, one of those who preferred enlarging facilities to creating new institutions, declared:

> Well, I think we have to [meet the increasing demand] through more institutions and also by increasing the institutions that we have. I don't see any institution in Pennsylvania right now that is actually too large. The present institutions can be increased.

A Kansas legislator said: "Ultimately I think we will have to expand. But I don't foresee that we will need any new institutions. I think we should take advantage of the facilities we have, such as the private schools." An Iowa legislator's comments were almost identical. Another Iowan worried about the expense of building a new campus:

> I have real reservations [about the new institution in western Iowa], but it happened to be a fact of political life we have to face. . . . It seems to me that it would be cheaper to expand one or all of the present institutions rather than start one. . . . [The new university] certainly has the potential to being a real drain on the overall appropriations to get it started, especially since we in Iowa will be financing it in capital and pretty much on a cash basis.

Many respondents, even advocates of enlarging existing educational institutions, noted limits of physical space and administrative efficiency and pointed to difficulties—such as student unrest—which tended to intensify when campuses became too large. A California committee chairman said:

> I'm not in favor of allowing the University campuses to get too large. I don't know what the optimum size is. . . . Maybe the optimum size is between 20,000 and 30,000. I think if you go beyond that you might be going past the point of diminishing returns, and then . . . conditions . . . enter into the picture that don't appeal to me. Having . . . large masses of individuals concentrated together in a small area, I think, contributes to the kinds of problems that we are aware of today on the campuses. . . . I would prefer to build up the newer [smaller] campuses.

PRIVATE INSTITUTIONS AND JUNIOR COLLEGES Although legislators generally did not give high priority to increased reliance on private schools as a means of meeting rising enrollments, many—especially in Pennsylvania and New York, which have a strong tradition of private higher education—viewed the development of these schools as an important supplement to the public institutions. A member of the Pennsylvania House declared:

> I think there's a place in the state both for private and state colleges, state-related institutions. I don't think that one should be developed at the expense or the sacrifice of the other. For instance, the private colleges in the Philadelphia area, Temple University and the University of Pennsylvania, play a very important and vital role in the development of our community down there. They accommodate a tremendous number of students and form an important part of the welfare and the health of the city. . . . Both institutions have to be encouraged to continue to grow and to accommodate our student bodies.

Another advocate of private schools, a New Yorker, told us that he was "strongly supporting the repeal of the Blaine Amendment to the [New York State] Constitution," because the amendment prohibited the state "from making any contribution to private institutions." Another New Yorker who emphatically endorsed state aid to private institutions declared: "I would give it directly to the institutions, and scholarship aid, too." A third Assemblyman agreed: "I would like to see the smaller private colleges brought up to standard so that they can carry a heavier load. They would be more attractive to better students."

Many state officials gave high priority to expanding junior colleges. As reported in Chapter 7, they saw many advantages to these schools—economy, accessibility to greater numbers of students, and curricula oriented to the basic vocational needs of individuals.

NEW CAMPUSES IN URBAN AREAS As noted, few legislators indicated a preference for constructing new campuses, but some felt they would be necessary—in the near or distant future. Of those who made specific comments in favor of creating new schools, most spoke of the need for more institutions in urban centers. One Texas Senator wanted to see "a new university in the San Antonio area." A Californian remarked:

> I would guess we will have to go to some new campuses, particularly in the urban areas. If we maximize the present campuses we have, many of which are simply physically outside of the commuter reach of much of our population, that presents a great drain on parents because they have to finance the living expenses of children who would be more economically served by . . . urban area campuses.

DIFFERENTIATION AND SPECIALIZATION A number of respondents suggested that the problem of enrollment increases might be handled through more efficient use of existing facilities, such as greater differentiation of junior and senior colleges, of undergraduate and graduate education, or of the subject matter taught in different schools. This specialization, in turn, would require more statewide coordination of existing universities and colleges. A California legislator, for instance, who expected campuses to become larger, emphasized the need for better organization of higher education on a statewide basis:

> Well, I suspect more than in the past that growth is going to have to be accommodated by larger . . . but also more effective campuses. . . . Although I think there are going to be new campuses . . . I think there is going to have to be a new reorganization. I don't think we can continue to simply add new University campuses, and at each state college four or five new liberal arts programs, and junior colleges. We are going to have to reorganize this whole system, because this added new growth is getting to be absurd.

One of his colleagues specifically advocated specialization:

> I think we're going to have to try to teach certain curricula in certain schools, and not try to teach a little bit of everything at all the schools, and let these students, to some degree, seek out the school that they can attend advantageously. I think we have to pool our resources on this.

A member of the Iowa House Higher Education Committee predicted greater differentiation between graduate and undergraduate institutions:

I see the state universities and perhaps some of the private universities decreasing in their importance in undergraduate training and increasing in importance in graduate training. The area schools may take up some of the pressure . . . by filling this gap of first two-year undergraduate training.

A Texas leader recommended greater differentiation between college preparatory and vocational-technical training programs in the junior colleges and concentration of graduate study in a few institutions. Another Texas legislator wanted to see at least four institutions offer graduate-level instruction only.

FINANCIAL EFFORTS For some respondents the problem of meeting enrollment growth in the colleges was simply a matter of finance. A Texan who favored increasing the number of junior colleges also favored better financing:

We are going to need more junior colleges to take care of this increase. I am in favor of upgrading the financial support of junior colleges from the state. Cities, as you know, are swamped by the demands for spending in the public schools. They will not be able to handle the problem of financing a junior college, and I think that it is therefore the state's obligation to help.

A Senator in Pennsylvania said: "Enrollment increasing can easily be taken care of, particularly with enlargement of the smaller colleges, if they had the finances. . . . I think we haven't hit the right sources of funds to pay for higher education."

An Iowa legislator, a member of an appropriations subcommittee on higher education, also felt that more money would be needed to meet the increases in enrollment, especially at the community college level:

I think there [are] going to be greater needs. . . . The birthrate is not near as great as it was during the forties, but I think a larger percentage of those that we have will participate in our education. . . . The last session . . . we were concerned, you know, about the amount of money for, well, advanced training in our doctor's degrees and master's degrees and such like. . . . We were concerned about the amount of money it was costing the state; where we could put, say, a freshman or sophomore, probably the four [classes] of them, for the same amount of aid. But I was educated to the fact that it's very necessary that we have these people to fill the jobs of professors and heads of the departments and everything. So I really don't know, maybe [we have] not come along as well as we could have in community colleges. I would say that was a place where we needed to expand. I personally feel that we need to do more.

THE FUTURE: LONG VIEW

Given the reluctance of elected officials to confront a distant future, it is perhaps not surprising that our question—"Now, taking a very long look ahead, say to 1980, what do you expect higher education to look like in your state?"—did not reveal much imaginative thinking.* In fact, apart from the many respondents who made the easy prediction of further increases in enrollments and increased state expenditures, those who said anything significant were in the small minority. While most respondents were generally optimistic, some were frankly pessimistic. Perhaps typical of the former was this legislator in Texas:

Well, we are going to be spending twice as much money as we are spending today, and we will have a larger enrollment. And I would hope that the standards in at least some of the schools will be upgraded. And I would like Texas to have more national recognition than we have had in the past. . . . I'd like to see us number one in the country. . . . I would say that we would have a much higher percentage of our kids in school by 1980 than we have today.

An Illinois Senator was both pessimistic and optimistic:

We'll still have our problems. . . . We won't be caught up yet in many of our programs, we won't have enough buildings . . . to meet our demand by then. We will still have young people wanting more in the way of higher education that will not be able to get it, just as we have now. But I believe that by and large in Illinois we are coming along better than most states. And I anticipate that we'll continue to do that.

*In justice to our respondents, this was the last question, and respondents may well have been exhausted. Moreover, as has been seen, we had previously asked at least two questions related to expectations of the future, one on "increase in demands for higher education," and another on master planning. Perhaps there was very little for respondents to say at this point without being repetitive.

Of great concern to some of the pessimists was the "curse of bigness" which, they thought, would accompany future developments. A California Assemblyman, admitted not having "given much thought projecting it that far ahead," yet speculated:

I would surmise that we're going to have pretty stereotyped systems of higher education. We're going to amalgamate all of the parts and we're going to be stuck with metropolitan type campuses in most instances, all too big. . . . We're going to blanket out opportunities for the private schools to flourish and grow. Those that are in existence will probably be able to survive, but there won't be many new ones created. And the state will dominate the scene as far as any new institutions are concerned.

Another Californian, a Senator, also anticipated increasing depersonalization of higher education:

My guess would be . . . that higher education will be much more of a businesslike operation and much less personal. . . . The huge campus of the 25,000 to 35,000 variety will exist and . . . the average age of the students, I think, will go up. I think you'll tend to find an older student body on these campuses as our international affairs take two or three years out of the boys' lives and as people get more in the habit of getting married, getting into the economy, and then figuring out what they want to do, and then coming back and going to school.

Along with growth in the size of individual campuses, a New Yorker predicted, "The whole system will become more monolithic." Another New Yorker's view was similar:

Well, about 80 percent of the students will be going to public institutions and 20 percent will be going to private schools. I would guess by that time the state will be doing a pretty good job of supporting both, probably through the students, rather than too much through the institution. A lot of colleges that are now private will be units of the State University, those that are marginal—the Buffalo route.

Expansion of Junior Colleges

In all states respondents saw an expansion of junior or community colleges as a long-range likelihood in the development of higher education. A member of the Illinois House speculated:

We'll probably have two or three more major four-year colleges. We'll certainly be rounding out the junior colleges with the whole state being covered. . . . Although I don't like it very well, I'd expect to see the state having taken over some of the private colleges.

Similar expansion was predicted by Iowa legislators. One said:

Well, I think you will see quite a great change in these area junior colleges. I think they will become . . . probably a good many of them, could become dynamic institutions of higher learning. It's even possible in isolated cases they could become four-year institutions. Here again is something we want to stay open-minded about. . . . I think you are going to see 70 or 75 percent college-age people going to some sort of post-high school training or learning of some sort whether it be arts, sciences, vocational, [or] technical by nature. . . . I presume there will be a continued expansion of graduate programs.

A Senator from Texas concurred: "There will be more development of the junior college network as well as expansion of the four-year colleges into new areas like San Antonio."

Changes in Teaching Methods A few respondents predicted dramatic changes in teaching methods. A Texas committee chairman, for instance, was quite emphatic:

I think that there will be . . . drastic changes in . . . the fields of instruction. We are going to see more and more use of computers, of educational television. I don't know but what we aren't going to be able to reduce the number of faculty members in the average institution. I think that the job of faculty member is going to be altogether different. . . . And I think that it is going to take less time for the average student to engage himself in his major study. In other words, it will be computerized. It will be on TV. . . . I have no reason to believe that the whole field of instruction won't be completely revolutionized.

Similar comments came from a Kansas legislator who contemplated that technical innovations in teaching might alleviate the need to drastically expand the number of campuses:

They will be using different techniques in instruction. Electronics will open up a wide area which is now open to a small degree. Teaching satellites and communications systems will be helpful. In Kansas there will not be any larger numbers of institutions. We may integrate and use the facilities on our campuses in a sort of satellite setting—using resources from one institution in other areas of the state.

A Louisiana leader made a similar projection:

I think that you'll probably see a complete revolution in the educational systems, the teaching systems. Use of the facilities for 12 months — which we have already tried in Louisiana — educational TV, closed circuits, teaching TV, that type of thing.

Only an occasional respondent predicted that there would not be much innovation in higher education in the next 10 years or so. Perhaps the most conservative statement came from the Kansas legislator who declared:

I think [education in 1980] will look about like it does now. I think its posture will be good, favorable, competitive. I don't think Kansans are going to let higher education down. Hoping that I know the basic philosophy of my fellow Kansans, I doubt that they are going to allow higher education to go off and become too innovative.

Some legislators anticipated improvements in teachers as well as in teaching methods and aids. Increased emphasis on teaching, as opposed to research, and improved teacher-training programs were predicted or hoped for. A New Yorker declared that higher education would be "much bigger" in 1980, and continued:

Perhaps more teaching and less research. This I say because I think industry can move into some of these [research] areas. . . . In order to cope with these huge numbers which we have to educate, I think that we will have a tendency to turn that way and let industry pick up some of this reasearch.

A Texas leader's projections were similar:

Very important I would say is the development of new emphasis on training of college teachers. Some Ph.D.'s know how to teach and some don't. . . . I think there is a need to develop more competence in teaching at the college level. Perhaps with some degree between the master's and the doctor's degree. That way those who are interested in teaching but not research can feel they are just as worthwhile as those who take the Ph.D.

Solving Social Problems A handful of respondents taking the long view thought that higher education would become more "practical" in orientation and that greater emphasis would be placed on solving current social problems. For instance, a New York committee chairman predicted:

I think . . . higher education is going to deal more and more with social problems in our complex society, trying to meet this problem in addition to just raising the standard of the economic product, so to speak. This is just what it was in the fifties—it was a meal ticket for a good job to start at possibly $5,500 or $6,000, go out, earn some money, buy a house in the suburbs, TV, etc. Now it is going to go in the direction of solving a concern for fellow men.

He expected more institutions of higher education to be located in urban settings, where they would play an increasingly important role in improving the quality of city life.

An Illinois legislator also predicted "more state institutions, more four-year institutions in some of the urban areas." A California Senator who was concerned with the problems of the ghetto mused:

If . . . I was calling the shots, I would provide open colleges as part of the suburban complex. I would provide subsistence grants on the basis of need, or a work-college kind of urban center. I would beef up the community colleges with state financing instead of complete dependence on local financing. I'd beef it up at the state level. I would recruit more minority professors into our system of higher education. And I would continue under the New York plan of developing a bigger and better system.

Asked if he thought these things could happen he replied: "I don't see it happening in the next eight years. But I think after this cycle of conservatism wears out, then we will move into another cycle. . . . I don't see it happening till about '75 or possibly '79 or '80."

Financial and Political Problems A few pessimists tended to project existing difficulties into the future. Especially financial problems, but also political conditions, were singled out. "By 1980," a Pennsylvania respondent said, "the financial problems ought to be insurmountable." Another Pennsylvanian felt similarly: "In 1980 the problem will be what it is right now—where is the money going to come from?" A Louisiana Senator thought: "The state-controlled systems are in just as much danger as the private systems when it comes to finances. I think we're in financial trouble."

The current failure of executive support for higher education was projected into the future by a California Democrat, who feared that his state's competitive position was declining:

A couple more years of this [Reagan administration] and we'll still be burrowing out in 1980. I'm not terribly optimistic right now. . . . When

other states are moving forward—like New York—in salaries particularly—
we're no longer in a position where we can always pick off the number
one guy in a department. . . . Starting now they pick off number 20 or so,
or 30. The impact of that sort of thing, and the kind of faculty that you
have, isn't felt immediately. It's felt after a few years.

A Senator from Texas foresaw the possibility of similar problems:

Well, I'm pessimistic. I don't know whether I ought to be or not. I'm pessimistic now with the governor's race shaping up like it is. If that Smith
gets in, nothing, including higher education and everything else, is going
to get any money beyond what they get now. It is going to be a long, slow
haul. . . . I don't see many encouraging signs.

CONCLUSION   The impression conveyed by legislators and state executive officials
as they anticipated the future was one of men beleaguered by the
pressures of office. Few of them seemed able to take a long view
that was wholeheartedly optimistic. Most of them were more aware
of possible difficulties in meeting the challenges to higher education
than of alternatives in coping with the expected needs. Most of them
seemed cognizant of the fact that the future depends on the present.
For all of them higher education was of necessity only one item on
the agenda of public policy making. And because it was only one
item competing with many others, few of these state officials were
willing to be programmatic.

Commentary

In the introduction to *State Officials and Higher Education,* the authors stress that they present a report, not a study. They carefully make a distinction between a report and a study to prevent the reader from deducing that the exposition is intended to reflect "a representative sample of respondents." The care with which the authors avoid generalization is a reflection of their scholarly and professional approach to the subject, an approach to be noted and respected by the reader.

Nonetheless, most informed observers of the state government scene will find that the material has great familiarity for them and the less experienced reader may appropriately infer that the report carries more significance as regards attitudes of state officials and legislators in general than the authors are willing to claim for it.*

The authors describe the importance of state legislators in higher education by noting that they are "strategic decision makers in politics affecting higher education. The resources mobilized for colleges and universities, the goals to which such resources are allocated, and how they are distributed depend to a great extent on the views and decisions of the nation's legislative bodies." On indirect influence, the authors continue, "legislators intervene in higher education not only through conscious planning but also through the inadvertent consequences of legislative action, or inaction, in such

*Obviously, in a volume of this length, with reports from so many people and so many authors involved, there is ample room for disagreement over details. For example, in the Illinois section, the use of the word "public" member to describe governor appointees is most unfortunate. It encourages the idea that trustees of institutions are not serving the public but are narrowly serving institutions. Clearly, this is not the case. In another instance, in my view, the author underestimates the public character of the Pennsylvania State University. These differences of view on usage and reference, however, do not alter the main points so skillfully drawn and so cogently expressed.

related areas of public commitment as agriculture, mental health, social welfare, or defense."*

In the public discussion of the funding of financial needs of higher education, to enable colleges and universities to meet their obligations and opportunities, it is sometimes assumed that the only institutions in serious financial difficulty are those which are privately controlled. Even some sophisticated observers loosely generalize that all the representatives of public universities need to do in procuring appropriations is to make requests to the legislatures. Any thoughtful perusal of *State Officials and Higher Education* will dispose of the point of view that the public universities are not also in serious financial trouble. Legislators and state officials are realists in tax matters, and they acknowledge a growing hostility to increases in taxes and show a general apprehension as to whether public spending can keep pace with inflationary costs. Further, they recognize that higher education, now requiring a large and increasing proportion of the total state outlay, is in competition with other demands on the state treasury—from elementary and secondary schools, hospitals and health services, highways, economic development programs, welfare, and emergency conditions ranging from urban problems to water pollution and environmental pollution. The legislator, even with strong and sympathetic interest in developing higher education, is troubled in the definition of priorities for state expenditure. That private higher education is also seeking public support adds to the difficulty of determining where the primary obligations lie.

The response of legislators on limitations of state resources provides a natural tie to the Carnegie Commission's report, *Quality and Equality: New Levels of Federal Responsibility for Higher Education.*

In discussing federal support, it is encouraging to note that most legislators see the need for such assistance as a supplement to state expenditure, not as a replacement. There is no reason to assume from the interviews here presented that the states will lessen their involvement with higher education. That they need help, however, even in the wealthy states, comes through clearly in the interviews.

*The inadvertent application of legislation to higher education can be easily illustrated. In every state, one of the important tasks of university representatives is to follow all legislation to make sure that bills not intended to apply to universities but which in fact have consequences for them are discussed with the sponsors. In most cases, sponsors of such measures will alter them to eliminate undesirable consequences.

The question of federal assistance to higher education takes on particular urgency when the respondents deal with public problems whose solutions have high urgency and which are related to the potential contributions of higher education. Examples are: increasing educational opportunity for students from low-income families, increasing the production of manpower for the health professions, and underwriting research related to problem solving in urban affairs. Obviously, these subjects go beyond state boundaries and reflect national necessities. Reserved as are many legislators about the amount, nature, and method of federal assistance, they reflect genuine concern about the ability of the states to deal adequately with these large and important social questions of high urgency.

This volume opens with Clark Kerr's listing of 10 "points positive." These form the framework or context of the report. It would be an oversight, however, if this commentary did not identify some of the negative reflections which emerge from the interviews.

1   It is clear that legislators do not give a high priority to expenditures on university research. They are willing to let the federal government support research programs, and they understand the necessity of research, even so-called basic research, in fields visible to them in terms of human service, such as agricultural productivity, medical care, and engineering; but legislators have little understanding of the place of research in the education of graduate students and only a vague understanding of social science and research in the humanities.

This point is of great concern to the major universities as they project their growth at the advanced and doctoral levels and as they are called upon to meet society's demands for research scientists and doctorates.

Obviously, the legislative reaction here is dependent upon the public perception, or lack of it, and the gap between the universities and the public on this point needs immediate and effective attention.

2   The interviews support the opinions of experienced observers in legislative relations in emphasizing that legislators feel remote from the complex operations of a university, even in relation to finances. False impressions of so-called luxury spending, compensation of faculty for outside work, teaching loads, requirements for buildings—laboratories and libraries, particularly—are but a few

of the subjects where complete understanding does not exist and where there is little time in the deliberative process for conveying full information adequate to correct the false impressions or fill the void.

As a result, universities are dependent upon the general confidence of the legislature in the university governance. To the extent that confidence is undermined by specific "bad" examples or by an inadequate communication, to that extent will these factors influence financial support in serious ways.

3   The interviews make clear that the majority of legislators are more understanding of student unrest than the general public, particularly in the area of free speech and peaceful demonstrations. Restrictive legislation on these points has not resulted in very many states. Even proposals that appear undesirable are often motivated by a sincere desire to be of help.

There are two elements in the current scene, however, which legislators generally do not understand. One is disruption, coercion, and violence and what they regard as the weak or permissive university response to such behavior. The other is the involvement of some members of the faculty in the encouragement of students to harass or disrupt the university. The legislators have learned to respect the university in its work and to give it a considerable amount of freedom in its operation. They expect the faculty to show the same respect, and they do not accept faculty dissent when pursued to the point of public conflict. Furthermore, they feel very strongly that the use of the classroom or the campus by faculty members for personal political views is a violation of professional standards.

The chapter "Legislators and Academicians" is a perceptive discussion. The gap in understanding here emphasized is one of the troublesome issues for the future.

4   The subject of student unrest and related issues and problems is treated at considerable length. The chapter on this subject is timely and useful because it sums up most of the public attitudes which reach legislators and other state officials who hear from constituents on this topic more than on any other one.

As noted earlier, public officials are inclined to be more tolerant of student unrest than the general public, and they are torn between the pressure for restrictive and punitive legislation and their own appreciation of the complexities of the problem. This theme runs through the interviews and is somewhat at variance with the speeches of officials which take the headlines.

One point emerges clearly, however—the legislators will have little regard for giving students any significant role in decision making in areas where they have no continuing responsibility or special competence. On influencing the conditions of student life, legislators are sympathetic. On influencing what is essentially a professional activity, they have little patience and the extent to which universities yield on this point, to that extent will the universities endanger legislative confidence in their management capabilities.

5 The legislative support for the public service activities of the universities is encouraging. However, here lies a problem of deep significance because faculties which must staff the public service functions traditionally have given a low priority to their personal commitment. Furthermore, the academic value system for professional advancement does not give adequate recognition to those engaged in public service.

This point has relevance to the lack of legislators' interest in basic research. Encouragement is given to research which is clearly visible in problem solving in areas that are important to the respondents. Perhaps the research activity by university people can give greater emphasis to the areas of immediate public concern. A by-product will be the training of students in a way that will have more meaning to them in their field of employment, either in academia or in government or in the private sector.

6 If federal control comes to higher education in any significant way, it is not likely to come as a policy declaration from the Congress of the United States, nor will it come from any deliberate intent on the part of the Congress through legislation to exercise such control. On the other hand, every recipient of grants from the federal government can testify to the controls exercised by the executive branch, either through interpretations of the intent of Congress in a given case by the department concerned or by regulations of the department in implementing legislation.

The same point may be made in most states. The interviews here recorded support the concept that the "proper domain of the relevant agencies or the universities themselves" should handle "most aspects of higher education." On the other hand, the effort for internal control of universities by state agencies is an old struggle. With each new administration and each set of new officers, it is reenacted.

Devices and strategies for control of universities by executive departments of state government have multiplied in recent times by regional and national associations of state governors and legislative leaders. In "experience swapping" sessions, new ideas for the control of the universities have wider application. Furthermore, as costs of higher education have increased and as states are more and more pressed by increased levels of spending by all state agencies, the pressures for controls are intensified. Most legislators, however, recognize that the universities are in the public service just as much as the executive departments, that the institutions are not "vested interests" to any greater degree than are other state programs and that, by and large, they have been characterized by high-level professional management in contrast to the turnover in government agencies.

CONCLUSION   Many people unfamiliar with the governance of public universities assume that because the state government is deeply involved in decisions affecting state universities, "politics" unduly influence those decisions and that this condition precludes professional management.

Politics has two meanings in the American vernacular. In one sense, the word connotes narrow partisanship, "deals" made out of expediency in the garnering of votes, a "pressure-group approach" to legislation. The other use of *politics* applies to public decision making through the established legislative process. The application of the latter to higher education is entirely appropriate. Public money is being spent—it must be publicly accounted for and its uses must be publicly determined. This is no different from the governance of any institution in the public service, be it church or other private organization which is the beneficiary of public benefits.

The interviews here presented indicate that the legislators know the difference. In most states, education is "off limits" in the narrow partisan sense. One may find examples to the contrary, but the generalization is nonetheless valid.

In the chapter "Planning and the Future," the authors wisely observe that "public policy is a subtle blend of past experience, present conditions, and expectations of the future. It is generally recognized that the past constrains the present and the present constrains the future."

Here, we have a fundamental issue. Universities deal with the future—the future of students, the future outcomes of research, the future conditions for university work in service to society. Hence, there will always be a difference in emphasis between what the university seeks to do in making a contribution to the future and what people, through their representatives, view as the urgencies of the present. In my view, these differences are reconcilable. However, as the interviews indicate, how to achieve this reconciliation is a challenge to every public university. Further, this objective must be sought in a setting where higher education is, as the authors point out, "only one item competing with many others" on the "agenda of public policy making."

David D. Henry

References

Harris, Joseph: *Congressional Control of Administration,* Brookings Institution, Washington, D.C., 1964.

National Association of State Universities and Land-Grant Colleges, Office of Institutional Research: *Appropriations of State Tax Funds for Operating Expenses of Higher Education,* Washington, D.C., 1968.

National Science Foundation: *Federal Support for Academic and Other Educational Activities in Universities and Colleges, Fiscal Years 1963-66,* U.S. Government Printing Office, Washington, D.C., 1966.

Norton-Taylor, Duncan: "Private Colleges: A Question of Survival," *Fortune,* October, 1967.

U.S. Department of Health, Education, and Welfare, Office of Education: *Projections of Educational Statistics to 1975-76,* OE-10030-66, U.S. Government Printing Office, Washington, D.C., 1967.

U.S. Department of Health, Education, and Welfare, Office of Education: *Projections of Educational Statistics to 1977-78,* U.S. Government Printing Office, Washington, D.C., 1969.

U.S. Department of Labor, Bureau of Statistics: *Technician Manpower: Requirements, Resources, and Training Needs,* Bulletin No. 1512, U.S. Government Printing Office, Washington, D.C., 1966.

Wahlke, John C. et al.: *The Legislative System: Explorations in Legislative Behavior,* John Wiley and Sons, New York, 1962.

Appendix A: Interview Schedule

1 Let me begin with a very broad question: How do you feel things in higher education have been going in (state) over the past few years?

    a   As you see it, what are some of the major problems?

       If probe necessary: How about enrollment increases? How about financing?

    b   How pressing do you feel these problems are?

2 Do you expect much of an increase in demand for higher education in the next few years?

   If not: Why not?

   If yes: How do you think the state can meet the increased demand? Should existing state facilities be enlarged? Should community or junior colleges be expanded? Should more use be made of private colleges?

    a   Which of these alternatives seem most feasible to you? Why?

3 Higher education serves many purposes—liberal education, professional education, technical training, research, and public service. Do you have any preferences in this respect? Are some of these purposes neglected? How do you feel higher education is doing in these matters?

    a   How do you think these diverse purposes can be best served by the various types of institutions in the state?

       Important: Should graduate education, or certain graduate programs, be concentrated in one or two universities, or should this be spread more widely?

4 I suppose that many different colleges and universities make requests to you here in the Legislature. How are these requests brought to your attention? Are you generally satisfied or not satisfied with the way the needs of higher education are handled and brought to you?

   a Just how are the different requests coordinated? Would you like to see changes in the coordination? What improvements do you think could be made?

   b Are you satisfied with the way in which the master plan has worked in the state?

   Or, if no master plan: Do you think a master plan for higher education should be developed?

5 We are wondering about the present division of responsibilities between the state government and the university or college authorities. How do you feel about the amount of control the Legislature has over higher education at the present time? Is it about right, too little, too much? Why?

   Probe: May I be a bit more specific? How do you feel about the kind of budget review now in practice? Should the Legislature have more of a hand in setting admission standards? Do you think the Legislature should have more control over the curriculum? How about the construction of new buildings and facilities? Should the Legislature plan a greater part there? How do you feel about the appointments of officials to the governing boards of the colleges and universities? Are you satisfied with the role of the Legislature in making these appointments?

6 Do you feel that the Legislature is equipped to do a proper job of overseeing higher education?

   Probe: Are your committees able to do this? Do you have enough staff help? What do you see as the role of the executive branch in all this?

   Probe further: Do you think the executive or the Legislature can do a better job of overseeing higher education? How's that? Are there conflicts between the Legislature and the executive with regard to higher education? What are these?

7 Are there ways in which higher education facilities could be used more economically and efficiently? How do you feel about summer terms? How about size of classes? Should they be larger or smaller? Would central state purchasing help?

Probe: Anything else?

8   A lot of programs compete for the tax dollar. I want to ask a few general questions first. How willing would you say are the tax-payers in (state) to support higher education? And what about the other legislators here in the House (or Senate)? How willing are they in supporting higher education?

   a   What is your view of admission of out-of-state students? Should their admission be more restricted? How do you feel about raising out-of-state tuition?

9   Let us talk about some other aspects of financing higher education. How is the funding of higher education affected by the needs of other programs in the state?

Probe: Just how is it affected?

   a   Where do you think is more need for funding here in (state)— in the primary and secondary schools or in higher education?

   Probe: Is there much competition between the institutions of higher learning and the lower-level school systems?

   b   As far as higher education goes, where does the greatest need for additional funding lie?

   Probe thoroughly: In construction? Which kind? In student scholarships? In research? In faculty salaries?

   c   Speaking of faculty salaries, what is your feeling in the matter— is faculty salary adequate, too high, too low? And what about administrative salaries?

   d   What means do you see are available to increase revenue for higher education?

   Probe: Tax increases? Revenue bonds? Federal aid?

   e   Do you think that students themselves should pay a larger share of the costs of higher education?

   If not: Why not?

   If yes: What would be the best method to make students pay more?

10   Let me touch another problem: Do you think the present geographic location of the state universities and colleges is effective in meeting

future needs? Are there parts of the state where new institutions are needed? Is there a need for expanding particular facilities (like medical schools)? Land-grant colleges and universities did a lot for higher education. What do you think of the idea of "urban-grant" universities?

Probe: Do you see the urban university playing an increased role in the future? How willing would you say is the Legislature to finance urban extension services similar to rural extension services? Should this be conducted at one or two universities or spread out throughout the state?

11 Do you feel that the state's needs for professional training are being met? What about teacher-training needs? Is teacher training adequate or not?

   a Do you think the federal government has a special responsibility in regard to professional training?

12 Speaking of the federal government: Federal aid now comes in many forms. In general, how do you feel about federal aid to higher education? Do you have any view as to what kinds of federal aid are most beneficial? And what kinds do you feel might cause harm? Would you like to see changes in federal programs? What kinds of changes?

   a Should federal aid to the different state institutions be channeled through some central state agency?

   b What do you think the consequences would be if federal funds to state and private higher education were cut off or much reduced?

   c In your judgment, does federal money ease the burden of the state or does it simply make it possible for the universities to do things they otherwise would not do?

13 Let me suggest something else: There are rich and poor, good and bad universities. I wonder how you feel about these differences? Would you say this is inevitable? Or would you do something about it? What?

Probe: How about admission standards? Would more money help? In general, do you think inequalities are the case here in (state)?

    a   Would you say that everyone is entitled to a college education at public expense?

       If not: How would you determine who is qualified?

    b   Do you think special efforts should be made to make it possible for kids from low-income or minority groups to receive a higher education?

14   In your estimation, how does higher education in this state compare with other states? Are such comparisons ever made when you discuss higher education in the Legislature? Can this state afford to keep up with other states?

    a   Would you say that there is *in fact* much competition between the states in this respect? Does this competition unduly increase costs? Is there anything that can or should be done about it?

15   In connection with the competition between the state universities, I would like to ask you about the faculty. What about the work load of professors? Are the universities here able to attract and retain good faculties? What is your feeling about faculty participation in public affairs? Should they participate or stay out? Do you think that too many professors leave?

    If yes: Why do you think they leave?

16   We have largely talked about the public institutions. What do you feel is the role of the private colleges and universities in all this? How much do the private institutions figure in planning the state's needs in higher education?

    a   The private institutions are financially hard pressed. Do you see the state doing something about this? If the state were to provide financial assistance to the private institutions, should it have control over appointments to the governing boards? What about control over their budget or audit?

    b   Speaking more generally, what future do you see for the private colleges and universities here in (state)?

17   Let me shift to the local community. In general, what do you see as the virtues of the junior colleges? Do you feel the junior colleges help in meeting the needs of higher education? Would you favor expansion of the junior colleges?

If respondent is generally favorable: Do you consider the junior colleges economical? What other advantages do you see in them?

18 We are asking you all these questions because we know that legislators hear a good deal about education from their constituents and interest groups. From whom in your district are you most likely to hear about *higher* education? What are you likely to hear from constituents—I mean, what are their satisfactions or dissatisfactions?

19 There is much unrest among college students these days, and it seems to be a nationwide phenomenon. How do you account for this unrest?

Probe: Anything else? What do you think can or should be done about the unrest?

After you have given respondent a real chance to express himself: Do you think the unrest in the universities has an effect on the way legislators react to the needs of higher education? Just what do they emphasize? Are college authorities too permissive in their view? Do they favor use of the police if there are demonstrations? Do they favor new legislation? What kind of legislation? Or do they feel students should be given more of a say in university policies?

20 Just one more question: Do you think higher education has much of an effect on the economic development and welfare of (state)? Could higher education do more to stimulate the economy? In what areas could it be most helpful? How could this be done?

   a Now, taking a very long look ahead—say to 1980—what do you expect higher education to look like then in (state)?

Appendix B:
Letter of Invitation

The following letter was sent to 88 legislators
and 14 state executive officials in nine states.

CARNEGIE COMMISSION
ON THE FUTURE OF HIGHER EDUCATION

Clark Kerr, Chairman

Ralph M. Besse
Joseph P. Cosand
William Friday
David D. Henry
Theodore M. Hesburgh, C.S.C.
Carl Kaysen
Roy E. Larsen
Katharine E. McBride
James A. Perkins
Clifton W. Phalen
Nathan M. Pusey
David Riesman
William W. Scranton
Norton Simon

1947 Center Street
Berkeley, California 94704
(415) 849-4474

Dear Senator _____:

    I am writing to invite your cooperation in a matter of utmost
long-range importance to our country--the future of higher education.

    Early in 1967, the Carnegie Foundation for the Advancement of
Teaching appointed a special commission to study the future of
higher education in the United States, of which I am Chairman.

    During the next four to five years, the Carnegie Commission
on Higher Education proposes to study many aspects of higher education in the United States and to examine many of the perplexing
questions that confront our colleges and universities and the nation
as a whole.

    As part of this study, we would like to talk with a small num-
ber of key state legislators. We would like to get your views on
the situation of higher education in general as well as your views
on particular problems. We expect that the interviews will approx-
imate one to two hours in length. With your permission we plan to
tape record the conversation in order to insure an accurate tran-
scription of your views. Our conversation with you would be strictly
off-the-record. While we are planning to prepare a report on legislators' views of higher education, your comments and those of others
would not be identified by name. We would like you to express your
views with complete candor.

    Professor _____ of the Department of Political Science,
University of _____, has agreed to undertake the interviews
in _____ for us. Professor _____ will seek an interview
with you in the next few weeks. I hope very much that you will cooperate with us in this important undertaking and grant him some of
your valuable time.

Sincerely yours,

Clark Kerr

Acknowledgments

Many persons helped in this enterprise. Our greatest debt is to our colleagues at other universities, the political scientists who conducted the interviews and provided background information: Professor George R. Boynton, University of Iowa; Professor Richard Hofferbert, Cornell University; Professor Malcolm Jewell, University of Kentucky; Professor Robert L. Lineberry, University of Texas; Professor Herman Lujan, University of Kansas; Professor Nicholas A. Masters, Pennsylvania State University; Professor Robert Robins, Tulane University; Professors Robert Salisbury and John D. Sprague, Washington University; and Professor Alvin D. Sokolow, University of California, Davis.

Because most of the interviews were taped, the task of preparing the mass of material for use in this report was prodigious. For this contribution, we are grateful to Miss Jean Harrison. Mrs. Lois Renner attended to the secretarial tasks of the project with thoroughness and efficiency.

Last but by no means least, we thank the state legislators and executive officials who gave generously of their time and knowledge by participating in the survey. We hope this report will be as useful to them as to those who seek to understand them. The authors will be pleased if it helps to bridge the gaps in understanding between polity and university that at times confound the mutual relationship.

Heinz Eulau
Harold Quinley

Index